LONDON, NEW YORK, MUNICH,
MELBOURNE, DELHI

SENIOR EDITORS Jon Richards, Alastair Dougall
SENIOR DESIGNER Jane Thomas
ASSOCIATE EDITOR David John
ASSOCIATE DESIGNERS Nick Avery, Goldy Broad, Gary Hyde, Simon Oon
ART DIRECTOR Cathy Tincknell
PRODUCTION Nicola Torode and Martin Croshaw
DTP DESIGN Andrew O'Brien

First published in Great Britain in 2000; this revised edition 2003
Published by Dorling Kindersley Limited
80 Strand, London WC2 0RL
A Penguin Company

A CIP catalogue record for this book is available from the British Library.

ISBN 0-7513-4617-9

Colour reproduction by Media Development and Printing
Printed in Spain by Artes Gráficas Toledo, S.A.U.

ACKNOWLEDGEMENTS

Dorling Kindersley would like to thank the following people:

Mike Stewart, Mike Thomas, Ben Abernathy, Karl Bollers, Andrew Liebowitz, Chris Dickey,
Lili Malkin, and Chris Claremont at Marvel Entertainment Group, Inc.
Paul Smith, Carlos Pachecho, Mike Miller, Bernard Chang, John Romita Sr., Dave Cockrum,
Tom Palmer, George Perez, Bill Sienkiewicz, Terry Dodson, Brian Miller and Hi-Fi Design,
Mike Rockwitz, Dan Hosek, and Paul Mounts.
Stan Lee and Holli Schmidt at Stan Lee Media.
Tom DeSanto, Holly Beverley, Dustin Dean, and Steve Newman at Twentieth Century Fox.
DRi Licensing Limited, John Kelly, David Gillingwater, Michael Leaman and Lynn Bresler.

See our complete catalogue at
www.dk.com

FRENCH
HOME

FRENCH HOME

Josephine Ryan

with words by Hilary Robertson
photography by Claire Richardson

rps

LONDON · NEW YORK

To the memory of my parents, Daniel Ryan and Sheila Le Mercier, who inspired my love of Ireland, France, and antiques.

Designer *Pamela Daniels*

Senior editors *Miriam Hyslop*
   & Catherine Osborne

Location research *Josephine Ryan*
   & Jess Walton

Production manager *Patricia Harrington*

Publishing director *Alison Starling*

First published in 2007.
This edition published in 2014
by Ryland Peters & Small
20–21 Jockey's Fields
London WC1R 4BW
and 519 Broadway, 5th floor
New York, NY 10012
www.rylandpeters.com

10 9 8 7 6 5 4 3 2 1

ISBN: 978-1-84975-357-9

A CIP record of this book is available from the
British Library

The original edition of this book was
catalogued as follows:
Library of Congress Cataloging-in-
Publication Data

Ryan, Josephine.
  French home / Josephine Ryan ;
with words by Hilary Robertson ;
photography by Claire Richardson.
    p. cm.
  Includes index.
  ISBN 978-1-84597-450-3
  1. Interior decoration--United States. 2.
Interior
decoration--France--Influence. I.
Robertson, Hilary. II. Richardson,
Claire, 1969- III. Title.
  NK2002.R93 2007
  747.0944--dc22

              2007023215

Printed in China

CONTENTS

6   *Introduction –
Sourcing Antiques*

12   *The Elements*

     14   Furniture

     24   Architectural Details

     30   Colour

     38   Textiles

     46   Mirrors & Pictures

     54   Lighting

     60   Ceramics & Glass

     68   Collections & Display

78   *The Rooms*

     80   Kitchens &
            Dining Rooms

     96   Living Rooms

     110   Bedrooms

     126   Bathrooms

     136   Workrooms

     144   Outdoor Spaces

154   Source Directory
156   Picture Credits
158   Index
160   Acknowledgments

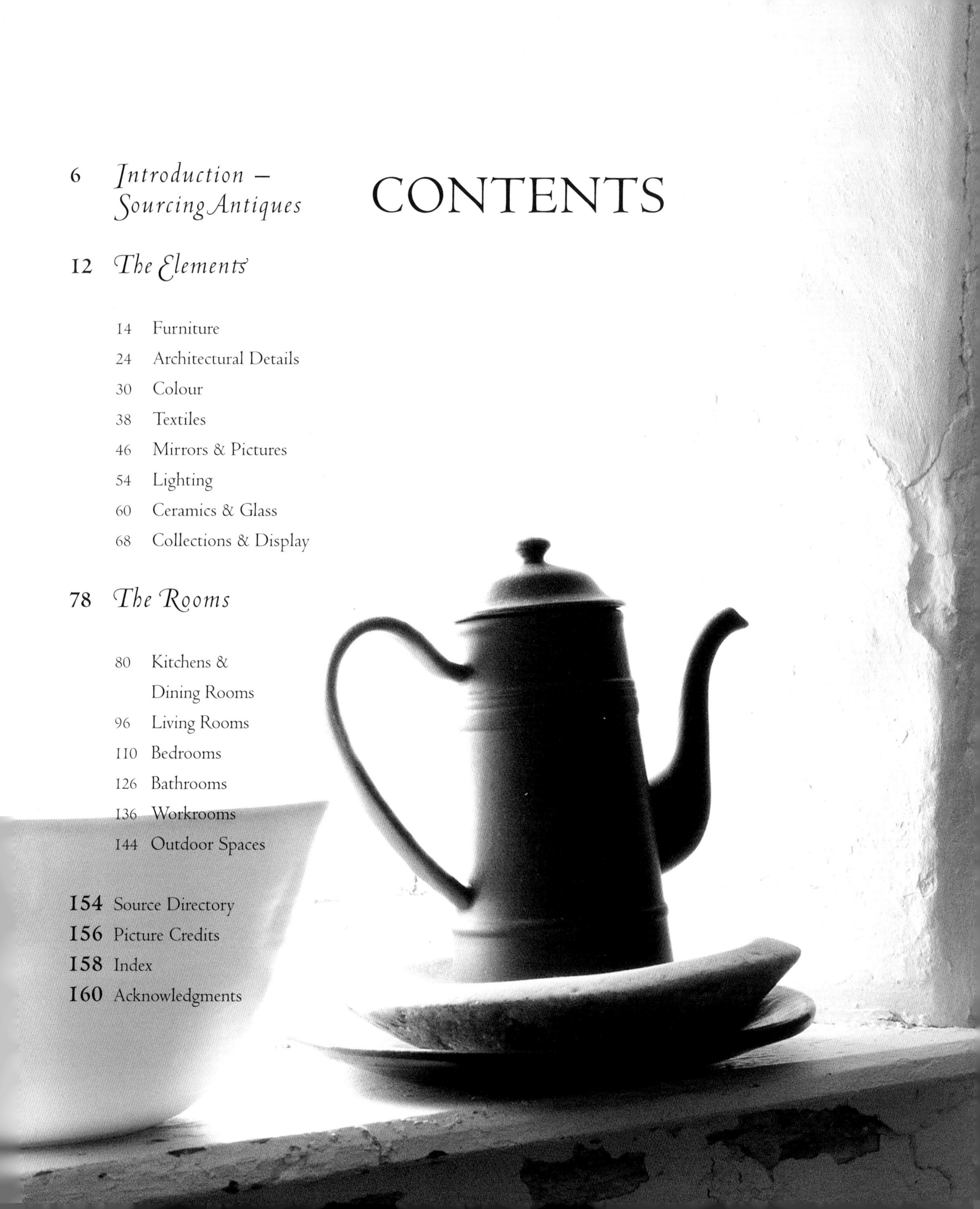

Introduction — Sourcing Antiques

HOW DO YOU SUM UP AN INIMITABLE SENSE OF STYLE? AND IS FRENCH STYLE, AFTER ALL, SO INIMITABLE? THE JAPANESE PHRASE, *WABI SABI*, OR 'PERFECT IMPERFECTION', SEEMS TO CAPTURE THE ESSENCE OF THE FRENCH APPROACH TO CREATING A HOME — THE CHEMISTRY THAT HAPPENS WHEN A LOOK IS PULLED TOGETHER WITH A CERTAIN NONCHALANCE UNDERSCORED BY ENORMOUS CONFIDENCE. IT'S AN 18TH-CENTURY SALON CHAIR COVERED IN SHREDDED SILK, TEAMED WITH A 1930S LUCITE® TABLE OR AN OVERSIZED CONTEMPORARY CANVAS HUNG ABOVE A ROCOCO CONSOLE. IT DESCRIBES A TOLERANCE, EVEN REVERENCE, FOR PIECES THAT SHOW THEIR AGE; A FEELING FOR THINGS THAT ARE AS BEAUTIFUL AS THEY ARE USEFUL. IT SUGGESTS THE SELF-ASSURANCE THAT EFFORTLESSLY COMBINES OLD AND NEW, THAT EMBRACES PERSONAL QUIRKS, INDULGES REFINED PREFERENCES AND REJECTS THE STERILITY OF SOULLESS DESIGN. THE IDEA THAT THINGS, HOUSES OR PEOPLE SHOULD ASPIRE TO PERFECTION IS RENDERED REDUNDANT BY THE WISDOM IMPARTED IN THAT ONE PHRASE — *WABI SABI*.

The hunt for treasures is a compulsive business. Unlike predictable high-street shopping, the pursuit for elusive vintage, junk or antique pieces requires research, discrimination, persistence, bargaining skills and not to mention taste. Language skills are also helpful if hunting abroad (although writing down your offer on a notepad also works!). Always take a calculator, a camera and a tape measure; the calculator to establish exact prices, the camera to take photographs of things you might pass by but come back to later, and the tape measure to ensure you don't come

LEFT & ABOVE The interior of Josephine Ryan's London shop is arranged in inspiring vignettes, the larger pieces of furniture accessorized with imaginative collections.

BELOW LEFT AND RIGHT
The shop front frames a 19th-century buttoned leather sofa and an oil painting by Clementine Fierard. A 19th-century child's highchair and a 19th-century doll.

www.josephineryanantiques.co.uk

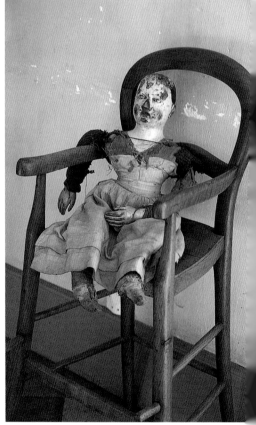

home with a white elephant. You may be hit by *le coup de foudre* ('love at first sight') and fall for something unexpected and utterly seductive that could change your whole shopping list. Beware of impulses, but be alive to chances of discovering extraordinary things. If you are putting together a look for your own home, carry a notebook with a record of your room dimensions. Also, don't forget to factor in the cost of transporting your purchases. Dealers should be able to arrange this for you or put you in touch with specialist transport companies.

If you are intimidated by the antiques world or fear that you are not knowledgeable enough, invest in some illustrated guides to antiques that will help you identify the pieces you find. The internet is also an invaluable tool and a good place to start. Search engines will direct you to websites listing auction houses, dealers and essential periodicals. *Aladdin* is the dealer's bible in France, *The Antiques Trade Gazette* in Britain and *The Journal of Antiques* in the United States. EBay is always worth consulting if you want something specific. There are also many architectural salvage websites.

Auctions can be overwhelming for the uninitiated, but are very thrilling when you are excited about a possible purchase and have a strategy! Attend the viewing, decide on your highest bid and stick to it. Don't jump in too quickly, but make sure that the auctioneer knows you are serious.

When combing France for antiques and junk it is useful to understand the correct terminology for the various outlets. A *friperie* sells antique bed- or table linen, while the *dépot-ventes*, found in every town, are warehouses full of furniture and accessories. *Brocante* and *vide-grenier* fairs are three- or four-day events held annually all over France (the one in Lille is reportedly the best). *Les Puces* are the Parisian flea markets held at the Place George Brassens, Porte de Montreuil and Saint-Ouen.

ABOVE An antique counter from a French shop acts as a desk at the back of Josephine's shop.

OPPOSITE, ABOVE LEFT
A pewter trophy and silver spoons.

OPPOSITE, ABOVE CENTRE
A butcher's block table teamed with an English Regency chair.

OPPOSITE, ABOVE RIGHT
A classical plaster figure of the muse of music stands on a rustic console paired with a trumeau mirror.

The

Elements

Furniture

INVESTING IN ONE IMPORTANT AND CHARACTERISTIC PIECE
OF FURNITURE — A DECORATIVELY CARVED ARMOIRE, A
PAINTED BUFFET, OR A CURVACEOUS CONSOLE TABLE —
WILL INJECT AN AUTHENTIC NOTE INTO THE SCHEME OF
ANY ROOM. A SKILFUL MIX OF OLD AND NEW — MODERN,
JUNK AND ANTIQUE FURNITURE — WILL GIVE THE
IMPRESSION OF AN INTERIOR EVOLVING OVER TIME.

THE EVOLUTION OF A HOME MAY INVOLVE ASSIMILATING
PIECES OF FURNITURE THAT HAVE BEEN HANDED DOWN
FROM GENERATION TO GENERATION. ACHIEVING THE
ECLECTIC LOOK IS ALL ABOUT CONFIDENTLY COMBINING
PIECES FROM DIFFERENT ERAS. FINISHES AND UPHOLSTERY
CAN ALWAYS BE CHANGED, WHICH SOMETIMES HELPS
TO UNIFY THE LOOK OF A DIVERSE COLLECTION. IF YOU
HAVEN'T INHERITED ANTIQUES BUT WANT TO BUY THEM,
DO SOME RESEARCH FIRST BY VISITING ANTIQUE EMPORIA,
HISTORIC HOUSES AND CHATEAUX. 'GET YOUR EYE IN'
AND LEARN ABOUT THE BACKGROUND OF PIECES YOU'RE
ATTRACTED TO.

OPPOSITE French chairs, even (or especially) those with shredded upholstery, specks of rust or faded paint, bring character to a room. There is something endearing about the way a rickety chair (even if it is missing a seat) is displayed – admired for its sculptural beauty rather than any useful purpose it might serve. The French don't think twice about bringing a metal garden chair inside or mixing styles of chair around a dining table. These decorative chairs have personality, and add a touch of flair to a room.

There are certain classic styles that immediately evoke the style of a French salon. A pair of Louis Quinze gilt *fauteuil* chairs will always add a certain elegance, but their shape is infinitely adaptable, working in both contemporary and traditional settings. Aside from function, the original purpose of the shape was to add sculptural style to the salon. The *fauteuils*, designed to be ranged against walls, echo the decoration of the *boiseries* (highly ornamented wooden panelled walls). Built more for comfort than the *fauteuil*, the *bergère* is a low upholstered feather-stuffed armchair originally designed to prevent a grande dame's skirts from creasing.

Designers are constantly reinterpreting these classics. Today you can find endless reinterpretations of the *fauteuil* – Philippe Starck's version for Kartell, the translucent 'Ghost' chair, is crisply modern and as light as air, while Maarten Bass' radical treatment, with its scorched wood frame and black leather upholstery, gives the chair a masculine edge. Trawling *brocantes*, flea markets and antique shops will yield *fauteuils* from different eras, from original to repro. The trick is to reinvent them according to your tastes and the role you want them to play in your home.

Matt paint finishes tone down decorative carving, while a slick of gloss paint in a daring shade combined with imaginative upholstery bring a piece of furniture boldly up to date (designer Paul Smith regularly puts his trademark spin on antique furniture in this way). Painted with a muted Swedish grey and upholstered in ticking or canvas, a chair will sit happily in an informal dining room or kitchen. Alternatively, a chair gilded and dressed up in silk taffeta will add glamour to a boudoir or sophisticated drawing room. Never be afraid of mixing contrasting styles together – antique with modern, rustic with sleek and the formal with the informal.

These quintessential chairs (*fauteuils* and *bergères*) with their curving lines, carved detail and decorative flourishes add a distinctly French flavour to an interior so that other pieces in a room can afford simpler, cleaner lines. The *canapé* (sofa),

THIS PAGE A symmetrical arrangement of French antiques gives instant character to a small bedroom where the plain walls and upholstered bed frame are balanced with a restricted amount of pattern provided by the floral quilt, striped upholstery of the chairs and simple striped linen cushion made from a grain sack. The *fauteuils* cleverly double as bedside tables, stacked with an assortment of hardback books and equipped with an elegant lamp.

BELOW A smart French marble-topped commode painted a soft Gustavian grey is toned down by its rustic setting. The vintage oil can is recycled as a vase.

OPPOSITE, TOP LEFT
The tapered legs of a long grey French occasional table have been cut down in size to create a stylish coffee table.

OPPOSITE, TOP RIGHT
A modern kitchen table has been upgraded to the role of console, somewhere to display interesting collections, such as textiles.

the chaise longue (daybed) and the *marquise* (love seat), though sinuously shaped and charming to look at, rarely provide the comfort and robustness offered by a traditional family sofa. Combining a generously proportioned contemporary sprung sofa with some more delicate antique pieces makes practical sense in a family living room.

Bargain hunters are bound to be attracted to the idea of a harlequin set. Look for pretty chairs (singly or in pairs) with a view to bringing them together as a group around a dining table. You might want to unify the shapes by painting them a single colour or upholstering them with the same cloth. Parisian painter Isabelle Rozot collects dainty black-framed Napoleonic chairs and upholsters the seats in different jewel-coloured silks. They move like chess pieces around her one-room apartment, adapting to the different social scenes.

The ubiquitous armoire is an adaptable free-standing wooden cupboard that can be used in any room in the house. In a kitchen or dining room it might store tableware, glass, cutlery or even food. In a bedroom or bathroom its shelves might be piled high with linen or folded clothes; it can even be adapted into a sort of home office filled with books, magazines and box files of paperwork. Some examples are painted, while others are made from pickled or plain woods. The doors may be glazed or mirrored (useful in a bedroom or smaller space). The buffet, a lower cupboard, is more likely to be stationed in a living room, dining room or hall. Sometimes it has two levels rather like a dresser, and the upper section forms shelves or a smaller cupboard. Like the armoire, it is often painted and sometimes elaborately. A smaller type of larder, a *garde manger*, is usually fitted with chicken wire fronts so that the contents are visible. These are especially well suited to an unfitted kitchen.

When it comes to furniture, the French are very casual about the boundaries between inside and out. A classic garden chair, similar to the ones you see in Parisian parks, might just as easily appear in a kitchen, a bathroom or bedroom. The same goes for the round café table that is often used throughout the house, even as a bedside or lamp table.

During the 18th century there was a trend for painting furniture to fit in with the overall scheme of a room.

THIS PAGE, BELOW LEFT
A painted buffet with chicken wire doors provides storage for glassware, and a surface to display tureens and vases of blooms.

THIS PAGE, BELOW RIGHT
The monochrome still life; religious prints, iron church candlestick and wooden gourd echo the muted tones of a plain painted buffet.

Motifs used on walls were repeated on furniture. As 18th-century craftsmen favoured softer, less expensive and less durable woods for the furniture they made to be painted, many earlier pieces have not survived. In the early 20th century, famous interior designers Syrie Maugham and Elsie de Wolfe, weary of the heavy, dark wooden furniture (known in the trade as 'brown' furniture) began to favour painted pieces because they appreciated the lightness of touch they brought to a room. More recently, Rachel Ashwell's feminine Shabby Chic look has popularized French and Gustavian painted furniture and many manufacturers are reproducing armoires, beds, *fauteuils*, and dressing tables in classic shapes. There are also companies that make 'blanks', unpainted pieces that can be finished to work with any colour scheme.

OPPOSITE A mixture of late 19th-century pieces; a drop-leaf chair, Biedermeier sofa and mirrored 1940s standard lamp conjure a sophisticated atmosphere in a Regency room.

RIGHT The uncluttered, rather austere dining room combines painted furniture, a Georgian corner unit and a Swedish bench, with a highly polished fruitwood table and an assortment of chairs.

BELOW A deeply-buttoned sofa, a *fauteuil* sporting lilac silk stripes and a pretty Louis Quinze side table make an interesting combination in a plainly painted room.

Architectural Details

A FRENCH ROOM WITHOUT A STICK OF FURNITURE WILL
STILL LOOK FRENCH. ALTHOUGH EVERY INTERIOR SPACE
BEGINS AS A BLANK CANVAS, AN EMPTY APARTMENT
OR HOUSE IN FRANCE WILL HAVE MANY IDENTIFIABLY
FRENCH FEATURES — WINDOW FRAMES, SHUTTERS,
DOOR FURNITURE, AND BALUSTRADES. THE PROPORTIONS
AND LAYOUT OF ROOMS ARE SPECIFIC TO VERNACULAR
STYLE. IF LIVING IN FRANCE ISN'T AN OPTION, THERE
ARE WAYS OF SUGGESTING AND EVOKING 'FRENCHNESS'
THROUGH COLOUR, FURNITURE, TEXTILES, FLOORS,
MOULDINGS AND ACCESSORIES. FRANCE HAS A CLEAR
VISUAL DESIGN VOCABULARY, WHICH WE CAN'T HELP
ABSORBING THROUGH FINE ART, ILLUSTRATION AND
PHOTOGRAPHY. THE MAISON PARTICULIER IN LUDWIG
BEMELMANS' *MADELINE* BOOKS, THE PARISIAN APARTMENT
IN A *NOUVELLE VAGUE* FILM, AND THE OVERBLOWN STYLING
OF SOPHIA COPPOLA'S VISION OF VERSAILLES IN HER
BIOPIC, *MARIE ANTOINETTE*, ALL SERVE TO ILLUSTRATE
FRENCH ARCHITECTURAL STYLES.

ABOVE LEFT A vaulted ceiling and decorative 18th-century panelling. The cartouche design depicts a scallop shell.

ABOVE RIGHT Panelling embellished with hats, garlands and bows.

OPPOSITE TOP LEFT Italianate panelling and a Louis XV fireplace in a French nobleman's house.

OPPOSITE, TOP RIGHT An internal courtyard with a beautifully vaulted stone staircase.

OPPOSITE, CENTRE RIGHT A Louis XV fireplace, trumeau mirror and trumpet.

OPPOSITE BELOW Locks on doors make interesting period features. The lock on the left is engraved with a fish.

In the 18th-century room the *boiseries*, carved sections of panelling that lined the walls, gave even unfurnished space definite character. Niches, alcoves, recesses and chimney pieces were incorporated into the whole design and sometimes a fitted armoire or bookcase might project from the panel or fill the space between the wall and the chimney breast. A niche might have a domed ceiling or be hung with a mirror, while alcoves with glazed doors provided space for storage and somewhere to display decorative objects. A bed

was often tucked into a recess, making a cosy retreat. Formal and organized, the shell of the room was then ready for furniture, but even bare it already had a very finished and homogeneous look. Elegant *manoirs* and chateaux may have preserved these beautiful bones, but they are no longer necessarily furnished with the same rigidity as an 18th-century room (with the *sièges meublants* and *sièges voyants*). However, the historic backdrop works very successfully with modern furniture or an eclectic mix of old and new.

OPPOSITE A 1699 stone staircase with balustrades.

ABOVE LEFT Natural light floods a staircase and its Gothic balustrades.

ABOVE RIGHT An austere stone staircase with thick rope handrail.

BELOW LEFT Two shades of pigment add character and warmth to a large stone stairwell.

BELOW RIGHT Wide bull-nose steps lead up to a grand panelled door.

In the absence of your own chateau, you might experiment with ingenious ways of re-creating or borrowing some of these architectural devices. Authentic materials and reclaimed architectural antiques are easily found at salvage yards and installing sections of panelling, doors, decorative ironwork, windows, parquet floors and fireplaces is fairly straightforward if their scale is compatible with the scale of your home. Double doors still covered in original paint colour, the kind that lead from one room into another, add an instant dash of French style to a two-room reception area. Reclaimed doors from armoires can also be used to make kitchen cabinets and other storage solutions. Whole rooms of boiseries can sometimes be bought from reclamation yards and relocated in a room with plain walls. Herringbone parquet, terracotta tiles and limestone paving are tactile materials commonly used for floors in France. Employing these classic textures will also evoke the feel of a French home.

Colour

THE FRENCH HAVE A RELAXED ATTITUDE WHEN IT COMES
TO REDECORATING, BEST SUMMED UP BY THE PHRASE
'BENIGN NEGLECT'. IF THEY WERE MORE INCLINED TO
REPAINT THE EXTERIORS OF THEIR HOUSES, WE WOULD
MISS THE UBIQUITOUS BUT CHARMING POSTCARD IMAGES
OF DISTRESSED AND PEELING PAINT ON DOORS, WINDOW
FRAMES AND WALLS. IN FACT, SUCH IS THE CONTEMPORARY
PENCHANT FOR ARTFUL DISTRESS THAT ACHIEVING THE
LOOK HAS BECOME A CAREER FOR THOSE ADEPT AT
DECORATIVE PAINT FINISHES. THE TRICK IS TO PRODUCE
A SURFACE THAT LOOKS LAYERED — AS IF ONLY TIME
ITSELF COULD PERFECT THE PROCESS. A 'FINISH' BEGINS
WITH A BASE COAT OF FLAT COLOUR, WHICH MAY BE
COVERED BY THIN, MILKY WASHES OF A COMPLEMENTING
SHADE, AND FINISHED WITH ANTIQUE WAX — BLACK
THAT THINS TO A DIRTY FILM DESIGNED TO SETTLE
INTO NOOKS AND CRANNIES, EMPHASIZING RATHER
THAN HIDING IMPERFECTIONS.

In our renovating- and decorating-obsessed world, swapping paint chip names and codes has become an international pastime. While some closely guard their favourite paint recipes, others become evangelical when they have finally formulated the 'perfect' shade of off-white or not-too taupe.

Fashion journalist and novelist Maggie Alderson holds that there are fundamentally two types of people when it comes to colour for interiors. Those who always opt for intense 'rainbow' colours and their polar opposite, the sophisticates, who abhor anything too chromatic, preferring the subtlety of the more complex, closely related shades she

terms 'mouse' colours. These are analogous colours, adjacent to each other on the colour wheel, that evoke a soothing, harmonious atmosphere.

The briefest glance at the interiors on these pages will leave you in no doubt as to which camp the French decorator belongs. The palette that predominates is of the chalky, subdued hues and tints, described so well by a Farrow & Ball paint chart – Dead Salmon, Bone, Drab, etc. The offbeat names say it all. Imagine blues merging into greys and greys into browns, and pale eau de nil greens deepening to become verdigris. In the French room white is never brilliant white as

OPPOSITE, LEFT In a neutral bathroom that combines vintage finds with off-white walls, the wooden floor and the rough outer side of the bath add some texture and warmth.

OPPOSITE, RIGHT Glass cake stands laden with green limes and grapes introduce a fresh, contrasting note to the two-tone Gustavian grey colour scheme.

THIS PAGE Employing a two-tone grey finish is an effective way of using darker, stronger colours in small doses. A charcoal grey band, painted up to dado height teamed with a paler shade, provides graphic background for the decorative Swedish sofa-bed and this painting on canvas.

ABOVE LEFT A bright, yellow-painted window frame adds a splash of colour to this white-walled room.

ABOVE RIGHT The yellow ochre paint above the panelling brings a flash of warmth to this room, an unusual contrast to the usual sober greys.

CENTRE, LEFT A pansy – the perfect combination of bright saturated colour combined with a dark off-black centre.

BELOW LEFT A Mediterranean bathroom mixes related shades of yellow, ochre and rust. These hot colours offset the utilitarian fixtures and fittings making the space feel welcoming.

BELOW RIGHT Matt pale blue/grey shutters and rough pigmented walls are a classic combination of warm and cool tones used in the south of France.

OPPOSITE There are particular shades that will always be associated with the south of France – a yellow ochre, a pinky terracotta or a cornflower blue. Accents of these shades bring warmth and relaxed rusticity to a room (reminiscent of interiors depicted in many Impressionist paintings).

ABOVE The dark grey band works as a counterpoint to the terracotta upper section giving the room a contemporary feel.

OPPOSITE (CLOCKWISE) The coolness of raw plaster walls and a terracotta tiled floor is offset by colourful cushions. Red anemones bring a lively accent to a neutral interior. Rich velvet cushions add opulence to a muted colour scheme. A bright red upholstered chair contrasts with the grey of this marble fireplace. Grey and chocolate tones are lifted by the whimsical lamp and the terracotta above the painted dado stripe.

it is tempered by the addition of black or raw umber. The interior schemes that combine these shades are marked by a lack of contrast. You certainly won't find strongly coloured walls teamed with gleaming white skirting boards. Instead, a warm grey might be used on woodwork and a related but deeper or lighter shade used around the walls. Fabrics, textural versions of the paint colour, add interest and depth.

These are the subtle tones that Italian painter Giorgio Morandi mixed again and again for his mesmerising still lifes. They remind us of the natural world where subtle shifts occur from moment to moment; they evoke dusk, a winter sea, or a stormy sky. Warm neutrals work as a soothing, uncomplicated backdrop to decorative antique furniture (less harsh than crisp whites). Employing these self-effacing shades allows textures of wood, metal, gilt, and tactile fabrics to take centre stage. Since the 18th century, the French have demonstrated a fondness for painted furniture. The colours chosen, frequently Gustavian greys or blues, work well with their complements

but next to clearer, stronger shades, these subtly patinated pieces would lose their mystery and merely appear tatty.

Choosing colours is a very personal process, but by asking some key questions you may arrive at a colour prescription for your space. Examine the quality of light in a room; a warm direct southern exposure differs markedly from a cooler northern exposure. What colour is the floor? As it is often the surface that receives the most direct light and acts as the greatest reflector, painting it a pale shade might significantly increase the ambient light in the room. How do you want to feel in the room? Do you use the space more at night or during the day? Even if you decide to paint your whole house white, you may want to play with warmer and cooler versions of the colour according to the orientation of different rooms.

Strategic use of colour can help mask flaws or highlight architectural details. Flat paint will tend to make surfaces visually recede, giving the illusion of depth, while glossier finishes appear brighter and attract the eye.

Textiles

THE FRENCH HAVE DEVELOPED A SIGNATURE STYLE WHEN USING TEXTILES IN THE HOME, NOT SURPRISING AS FRANCE HAS ALWAYS BEEN IN THE VANGUARD OF TEXTILE DESIGN. PERHAPS THE MOST RECOGNIZABLE PRINT IS THE *TOILE DE JOUY*, WHICH INSTANTLY EVOKES THE ESSENCE OF A FRENCH INTERIOR — AND IS TO FRENCH DECORATING WHAT FLORAL CHINTZ IS TO ENGLISH. ALTHOUGH ONCE SPECIFIC TO FABRICS PRODUCED BY CHRISTOPHE-PHILIPPE OBERKAMPF, THE TERM *TOILE DE JOUY* NOW APPLIES TO ANY FABRIC PRINTED WITH A MONOCHROME FIGURATIVE DESIGN. OBERKAMPF OPENED UP HIS FIRST PRINT WORKS IN 1760 AT JOUY-EN-JOSAS, A VILLAGE ON THE OUTSKIRTS OF PARIS. BY 1797, THE DEMAND FOR *TOILE DE JOUY* HAD BECOME SO HIGH THAT OBERKAMPF'S PRINT WORKS WERE PRODUCING 5,000 YARDS OF PRINTED CLOTH A DAY. OBERKAMPF AND HIS DESIGNER CHRISTOPHE HUET ENJOYED GREAT SUCCESS. MARIE ANTOINETTE DECORATED VERSAILLES WITH THESE UNOSTENTATIOUS, MONOCHROMATIC FABRICS, AND THERE IS A MUSEUM IN JOUY-EN-JOSAS DEVOTED ENTIRELY TO *TOILE DE JOUY*.

ABOVE In an attic bedroom a metal campaign bed is piled with a collection of vintage floral *boutis* and quilts.

OPPOSITE The mood of a plain and simple bedroom is lifted by a vintage floral quilt in soft shades of red and taupe.

The *toiles* originally came in several subtle colours – a rose madder, a greyish blue, a mauve and a brown. Nowadays they are reproduced in many other shades and are regarded as a classic choice for both traditional and modern settings. Recently, design duo Alistair McAuley and Paul Simmons of Timorous Beasties produced a *toile* design that depicted a tongue-in-cheek rendering of a contemporary urban scene. Although their work is certainly a unique and appealing twist on the traditional vistas portrayed on *Toile de Jouy* from the 1800s, these classic scenes have not lost their charm. Antique pieces of *toile* are very collectable, and sometimes even the smallest fragment will be preserved as part of some larger project or as a cushion, pelmet or runner. The French do not hesitate to use this and other fabrics as a wall treatment, stretched onto wooden wall battens.

The rose madder colour, frequently seen in combination with a neutral tone, is printed on many other floral fabrics that are mixed and matched very effectively in country houses (an essential ingredient in the shabby chic look). Antique quilts or *boutis* made with fragments or whole lengths of 'indiennes' (calico and chintz printed with simple floral and geometric motifs) and *toiles* are sought-after items, but new ones are still made and easily found. The ubiquitous *boutis* is used all over the French home as a bedcover, throw, tablecloth and even as a warm, draught-excluding curtain. The French knack for reinvention has also been applied to the monogrammed linen wedding sheet, which appears in many guises. There are some who seem to seek only to launder, order and display their collections in expertly folded piles, while others employ them as unlined curtains, cut them up to make cushion covers and loose covers or drape them over their dining tables. Linen dealer Jane Sacchi dyes some of the sheets she finds with woad. The blue pigment produces shades (of varying intensity) similar to the colour of cornflowers that combines perfectly with the other staple of the relaxed French home, ticking.

OPPOSITE A laundered stack of linen sheets in neutral colours doubles as a sculptural display on a metal garden table.

ABOVE LEFT A deep frill transforms this basic shelf into an informal wardrobe. Hung with vintage shifts, it becomes as pretty as a boutique.

ABOVE RIGHT A fruit picker's ladder makes the ideal place to display and store tablecloths, napkins, pillowslips and sheets.

RIGHT Vintage cotton reels, lace and beads coil together forming a textural still life.

The French could not achieve that breezy, effortless weekend house look without using stripes. In classic colour combinations of indigo with cream or white, red and taupe or grey, they are employed indoors and out, teamed with florals or other stripes. Vintage mattress tickings are collected and archived with the same reverence as *boutis* and *toiles*. These staples can be effectively combined with the plainest linen, canvas or calico. A decorative pelmet might be paired with unadorned curtains or embroidered monograms from wedding sheets recycled as a panel on a cushion or a feature on a slip-cover.

LEFT A plain linen curtain with a deep floral band replaces the door to a bathroom, where a light muslin drape falls from a hinge.

OPPOSITE, TOP LEFT Textiles are used effectively to soften this hallway; a sacking runner hangs artfully over the metal console, a richly coloured rug breaks the geometry of a tiled floor, and a diaphanous two-tone curtain breaks the hard lines of the door frame.

OPPOSITE, TOP RIGHT A thick satin calamine pink counterpane makes a handy draught-excluding curtain.

OPPOSITE, BELOW RIGHT Pieces of antique *passementerie* are left out on display.

OPPOSITE, BELOW CENTRE The traditional floral chintz lampshade is an unlikely companion for an old oil canister.

OPPOSITE, BELOW LEFT A kilim thrown over a table gives the room a shot of rich colour.

Mirrors & Pictures

THE MIRROR IS ONE OF THE WORLD'S OLDEST ACCESSORIES.
FOR CENTURIES ARTISTS AND ARTISANS EXPERIMENTED WITH
VARIOUS MEDIA — BRONZE, SILVER, GOLD, IRON PYRITES,
VOLCANIC GLASS AND ROCK CRYSTAL — IN AN ATTEMPT TO
REPRODUCE THE QUALITY OF CALM WATER, MAN'S FIRST
EXPERIENCE OF THE REFLECTED IMAGE.

THE INVENTION OF MIRROR PLATE IN THE 14TH CENTURY
ALLOWED MIRROR MAKERS TO PRODUCE FLAT, COLOURLESS
GLASS. IN THE LATE 17TH CENTURY THE FRENCH INVENTED THE
CASTING METHOD, WHICH LATER ENABLED MANUFACTURERS
TO PRODUCE MIRRORS ON A MUCH LARGER SCALE. IN THE
MID 18TH CENTURY THE MIRROR BECAME AN ARCHITECTURAL
DEVICE, AN INGENIOUS WAY OF REFLECTING LIGHT AND
MAGNIFYING SPACE. EMPLOYED IN 'GALLERIES', ROOMS USED
FOR BALLS AND BANQUETS AND IN 'CABINETS', SMALL ROOMS
KEPT FOR CONVERSATION, MIRROR PLATE WAS SET INTO
PANELLING OR GESSO FRAMES AND EVEN CEILINGS WERE
DECORATED WITH IT. THE MOST FAMOUS EXAMPLE, THE HALL
OF MIRRORS AT VERSAILLES, WAS COPIED ALL OVER EUROPE.

OPPOSITE, TOP A collection of black and white prints hung in a group smartens a white tongue-and-groove panelled stairway.

OPPOSITE, BELOW LEFT A painting of an angel gives this bedroom a feeling of serenity.

OPPOSITE, BELOW SECOND LEFT The 1950s portrait of an unknown man suggests the historical feel of a Bloomsbury drawing room.

OPPOSITE, BELOW SECOND RIGHT Ancestral portraits hung above a daybed stand out against rough stone walls.

OPPOSITE, BELOW LEFT An 18th-century painting depicts an intimate scene of a woman in her bedroom.

RIGHT The still life in this painting is echoed in the arrangement of ceramics displayed on the cupboard below.

BELOW, LEFT A nude painted in the 1920s leans casually against the wall becoming part of a monochrome still life.

BELOW, SECOND LEFT Celestial cherubs in the heavens teamed with a Bagues wall light.

BELOW, RIGHT A framed sepia portrait displayed on a side table.

BELOW, SECOND RIGHT The print of an iris is a substitute for real flowers in a group of bottles.

Where light levels are low, a reclaimed factory window frame with a panel of mirror fixed behind it suggests a real window, and acts as a smart light-reflecting device, helping to brighten a dull room. Decorator Nina Campbell uses *trompe l'oeil* mirrors in her city garden, giving the impression of endless vistas.

Many antique French mirrors, from those with elaborately gilded gesso frames to the art deco styles, have 'foxed' glass (where the mercury silvering separates from the glass). This only adds to their appeal as they give back a smoky, atmospheric reflection. Similarly, *verre églomisé*, the term for gilded glass, has a flatteringly soft effect. Reproduction

THIS PAGE Vintage and modern mirrors of varying sizes and finishes have been hung in a row reflecting vignettes of the room beyond. Collections of mirrors work well in hallways and liven up darker spaces.

OPPOSITE, TOP LEFT

A simple 19th-century mirror frame, given a coat of matt black paint appears to frame the still life on the table.

OPPOSITE, TOP RIGHT

A plain white ogee mirror frames a selection of colourful Madonnas.

OPPOSITE, BELOW LEFT

A decorative 19th-century Venetian mirror hangs above a simple table and tole table lamp.

OPPOSITE, BELOW RIGHT

A carved French giltwood mirror is teamed with a modern ceramic vessel and antique silver candlesticks.

ABOVE RIGHT
Three round wooden frames with different finishes (originally windows) make a bold statement when positioned in a row like ship's portholes.

mirrors, with gilt rather than gilded frames, benefit from a coat of matt white or pale grey paint when brought together as a group.

The paintings that Josephine Ryan chooses rarely boast a grand provenance. Most are by amateurs, but they all share a sensibility, a particular tone or atmosphere. Still lifes in muted colours, reminiscent of Giorgio Morandi's work, are particularly suited to the subtlety and texture of antique French furniture. It makes sense to collect paintings that share a theme. So, for the kitchen, you might want to search for paintings that depict food or kitchenalia, whereas nudes are better suited to the intimacy of a bedroom or bathroom. Portraits of unknown subjects, on the other hand, have a certain mystery and enhance the sense of history, perhaps borrowed history, in an interior.

Smaller paintings, prints or photographs can be hung in groups. Otherwise a small, single picture looks best when hung low so that it connects visually with objects displayed on a table or leaning against a wall as part of a still life. Experts often advise using the floor to map out an arrangement of pictures before committing to the final scheme on the wall. If you are fond of change, you might experiment with long shallow shelves with a lip, intended for several pictures to line up at a slight angle. These displays can be changed easily and are perfect for mixing varying sizes of frame and canvas.

Lighting

FOR CENTURIES FRANCE HAS PRODUCED SOME OF THE MOST
GLAMOROUS, DECORATIVE AND INNOVATIVE LIGHTING. THE
FIRST SIMPLE CHANDELIERS WERE MADE TO LIGHT MEDIEVAL
CHURCHES, BUT 18TH-CENTURY DEVELOPMENTS IN GLASS-
MAKING ALLOWED THE LESS EXPENSIVE PRODUCTION OF
LEAD CRYSTAL. APPRECIATED FOR ITS LIGHT-SCATTERING
PROPERTIES, THIS HIGHLY REFRACTIVE GLASS BECAME THE
ESSENTIAL INGREDIENT IN THE DESIGN OF ELABORATE,
GARLANDED CHANDELIERS AND WALL SCONCES. CURVACEOUS
METAL FRAMES DRIP WITH JEWEL-LIKE DROPS OF FACETED
GLASS AND CRYSTAL, FREQUENTLY COLOURED IN SHADES
THAT MIMIC SEMI-PRECIOUS STONES SUCH AS AMBER,
AMETHYST, EMERALD AND TURQUOISE. THESE STYLES
OF LIGHT FIXTURE HAVE BECOME INCREASINGLY POPULAR
IN RECENT YEARS, PARTICULARLY EMPLOYED AS A PLAYFUL
CONTRAST TO SPARSE ARCHITECTURAL SPACES THAT EVEN
DIE-HARD MINIMALISTS CAN'T RESIST.

OPPOSITE Jam jars filled with night lights add a soft glow to the dusky light in a rustic courtyard garden.

THIS PAGE A grand hallway with a soaring ceiling is elegantly lit by rows of hurricane lamps.

ABOVE LEFT A large contemporary chandelier hangs from an historic vaulted ceiling.

ABOVE RIGHT A 19th-century metal frame hung with strings of light-refracting crystal.

BELOW LEFT An 18th-century church lantern slung low over a cupboard.

BELOW RIGHT Contemporary metal and glass lampshades (a style popular in the 1930s–40s).

Whatever your tastes, don't undervalue the importance of lighting and the role it can play in making a home feel good. Your rooms may be exactly as you planned, filled with a wisely judged mixture of esoteric and utilitarian items, the colours subtle and harmonious, the textures comforting and sensual, but if the lighting is wrong, the artfully orchestrated atmosphere will be ruined. Central lighting is often harsh and rather cold, and should be supplemented by table lamps that contribute a warm glow, uplighters, and directional lighting from anglepoises and extending wall lights (these work especially well as reading lights fitted on either side of a bed). Spotlights set into the ceiling are a discreet and minimal option ideal for bathrooms and kitchens.

Candlelight, although hardly an efficient way of lighting a room, produces a soft romantic mood perfect for dining rooms

and gardens at night. Rows of storm lanterns, tea light holders made from porcelain or glass and even jam jars can be used imaginatively to illuminate pathways or corridors. Candelabra and candlesticks are the ultimate in portable lighting.

Of course, before electricity, chandeliers were intended to be equipped with candles, not bulbs, and there's every reason to use them in the same way today. French designers have experimented widely with the chandelier; for example, Madeleine Boulesteix's ersatz creations may be assembled from recycled kitchenware, glasses, teacups and beads, but the effect is deceptively opulent. Even in the 19th century a chandelier frame might come in the fanciful form of a galleon, a hot air balloon or a birdcage.

The antique dealer's fondness for reinventing aesthetically pleasing but redundant objects or fragments is evident in many French homes. Old soda siphons, sinuous pieces of iron balustrade, architectural stonework, ginger jars and candlesticks have all been converted into inventive lamp bases and topped with a shade of some sort. An expert in surprising transformations, Lin Conor turned a French village's public address system (similar to megaphones) into pendant lights for her kitchen. She literally and metaphorically turns ideas on their heads! Such ingenuity is typical of the French attitude to decorative objects; they may always be reused, albeit in an unconventional way.

ABOVE LEFT A delicate 1940s mirrored wall sconce is fitted with candles instead of bulbs and decorated with beads.

ABOVE RIGHT An 18th-century silver-gilt carved wood chandelier hangs elegantly in a hallway.

Ceramics & Glass

A NATION THAT DEVOTES SO MUCH TIME TO PREPARING
AND EATING FOOD HAS NATURALLY DEVELOPED DISTINCTIVE
TASTES IN ACCESSORIES FOR THE DINING ROOM AND
KITCHEN — DECEPTIVELY SIMPLE TASTES, OF COURSE.
COUNTLESS CHEFS AND FOOD EXPERTS REFUSE TO SERVE
FOOD ON ANYTHING OTHER THAN THE PLAINEST WHITE
PLATES, AND SOMMELIERS ABHOR THE IDEA OF WINE
SERVED IN COLOURED GLASSES. WHY? BECAUSE THE NATURAL
COLOURS, TEXTURES AND ARTFUL PRESENTATION OF THE
FOOD MIGHT BE OVERWHELMED BY TOO MUCH PATTERN
OR COLOUR. IN THIS INSTANCE, SURFACE DECORATION IS
SUPERFLUOUS. NOTHING SHOULD DISTRACT FROM THE FOOD.

Armoires and buffets are stacked high with unembellished porcelain and faience (stoneware and earthenware) glazed in every imaginable shade of white or cream. Despite this rigour about colour, the French cannot resist adding a certain whimsical edge to their tables. Chic Parisian tableware company Astier de Villatte produce tureens, cups, plates and pitchers glazed in pure, translucent white, but their shapes would not look out of place at the Mad Hatter's tea party. The teacups and plates, in particular, resemble children's book illustrations, seeming almost two-dimensional. Their slightly

THIS PAGE, LEFT A wooden peg rail is put to use to keep a row of white coffee cups to hand.

THIS PAGE, BELOW A glazed kitchen cupboard contains a set of neatly displayed precious 1920s Wedgwood.

OPPOSITE, TOP LEFT
The slim, glass adjustable shelves of a vintage storage unit from a bakery are used to display a mixture of contemporary ceramics in different styles.

OPPOSITE, TOP RIGHT
Stacks of transferware plates are kept on a slatted garden chair.

OPPOSITE, BELOW RIGHT
A Georgian corner cupboard accessorized with simple cream porcelain bowls.

ABOVE A metal garden table scattered with *faisaille* pots — pierced earthenware used to contain a particular kind of cottage cheese.

OPPOSITE, TOP RIGHT Green glazed bowls and plates.

OPPOSITE, CENTRE RIGHT A group of glass apothecary bottles with an Irish stoneware vessel and a contemporary glass plate. The faded blooms freshen the neutral palette and add texture.

OPPOSITE, BELOW RIGHT The solid shapes of the opaque white Danish bottle and rounded ceramic vase unite an ethereal still life of differently-shaped clear glass pieces.

uneven, raw texture and absence of smooth edges adds to the impression of these forms having leaped straight from the page of the designer's notebook. However, a table dressed with Astier de Villatte still manages to appear deeply sophisticated; an apt example of that trademark French trick of fusing the naive with the decorative, to great effect.

Eighteenth-century taste in tableware was dramatically different. The Sèvres porcelain enterprise started in 1740 and encouraged by Madame de Pompadour, a well-known courtesan at the time, created lavishly embellished designs in rich colours – blue, magenta and gold. If this grand type of porcelain is used today, any hint of pattern is classic or subtle, usually limited to the edge of a plate and the rim of a bowl. Vintage transferware – the polar opposite of the excesses of Sèvres – is relatively inexpensive and widely collected, but looks more at home in the rural kitchen. The plain shapes are often printed with graphic two-colour motifs, often floral.

It's in the more rural areas of France where you will find the faience glazed a dark olive green, mustard yellow or rich cream. Rustic urns and jars, originally made as containers for olive oil, are used as decorative objects or somewhere to store utensils. Durable ovenproof cooking dishes and bowls are still used and look handsome stored *en masse* on open shelves.

The classic Duralex tumbler, staple of café and kitchen alike, is the ultimate in utilitarian glassware. It is used indiscriminately for coffee, cognac, wine and water. Otherwise

drinking glasses tend to be plain and simple. Glass cake
stands, cloches and decanters displayed in groups on shelves
and sideboards are more esoteric, whereas old apothecary
bottles make ideal vessels for displaying casual arrangements
of single stems and branches that the French are so fond of
having in their homes.

The French approach to setting a table is refreshingly
unpretentious. The restrained elegance of laundered linen,
white porcelain and sparkling glasses works as the most
effective backdrop for visually seductive food. A heap of red
cherries in a glass dish, cheeses on a board and a loaf of
bread are the ingredients that make the table look enticing.

Collections & Display

'THERE'S CHIC IN REPETITION' DECLARED AMERICAN
DECORATOR BILLY BALDWIN, AN ADVOCATE OF THE
CAREFULLY CURATED COLLECTION WHO ENCOURAGED
HIS CLIENTS TO INTEGRATE PERSONAL TREASURES INTO
HIS SCHEMES RATHER THAN BANNING THEIR PECCADILLOS
TO THE ATTIC. 'NOTHING IS INTERESTING UNLESS IT IS
PERSONAL,' PROCLAIMED BALDWIN SAGELY. TOO MANY
MODERN OR MINIMALIST SPACES FALL INTO THE TRAP OF
LOOKING SOULLESSLY PERFECT, MORE LIKE A HOTEL ROOM
THAN A REAL HOME. BALDWIN WAS DELIGHTED UPON HIS
RETURN TO A ROOM HE HAD DECORATED TO FIND IT
'CUSTOMIZED' BY ITS OWNERS.

Authentic collections should be assembled over time, not bought by the yard as the arriviste buys leather-bound books. Choosing objects that have meaning, but not necessarily great value, can add significant charm to a room. A collection of milk jugs and pitchers in every shade of white, a selection of shop-front characters in various typefaces, fossils, mercury glass, crucifixes, plaster madonnas, globes, candlesticks, even postcards can all be employed to reinforce a sense of the personality alive in your home. If you have a theme in mind, then visits to flea markets, boot fairs and junk shops will be far more focussed.

Displaying your treasures affords the opportunity to bring subtle but refreshing changes to a particular room. Flowers, branches and grasses add a natural and seasonal vitality to groups of vessels. These still lifes need not remain static – move things around, expand or contract groupings, and restyle open shelves or glass-fronted cabinets. If you lack inspiration, consider a still-life painting by Giorgio Morandi or Paul Cézanne who by grouping the most banal objects revealed their intrinsic beauty. Morandi, who lived and worked in the same living room throughout his career, arranged his compositions from an unchanging stock of vessels, vases, jugs and bottles, and yet every painting reveals something unexpected, a new relationship between each object. Study how light falls in your space and gather diverse shapes that cast sculptural shadows from window-sills drenched in sunlight.

'It is ordinary to love the marvellous; it is marvellous to love the ordinary', wrote Donald Windham of his friend Joseph Cornell's work. Cornell filled boxes with objects that people usually leave forgotten in musty drawers or toy boxes – clock faces, corks, maps, photographs. By choosing to display these abandoned objects he invested them with mystery. For an original collection or display, experiment with groupings of things that might usually be hidden in a trunk or jewel box. You'll be surprised how much an arrangement of unusual objects adds interest to a room.

OPPOSITE Most collections start with a personal passion – 17th-century carved wood Madonna and child, a plaster image of Christ (under a glass dome), a Spanish Child of Prague and crucifixes made from glass, silver, ivory and cut steel, diamonds and crystal, are gathered together and shown in groups on tables, window-sills and mantels.

ABOVE A raft of decorative Indian silver bowls.

CHIEN LUNATIQUE

ABOVE Display favourite objects with a sense of humour!

ABOVE RIGHT Themes help focus still lifes. Here, a herd of vintage animals, escapees from a toy box, line up along a shelf.

When attempting to order collections on sideboards, consoles, dressers, *étagères* and mantels, you are bound to find that some objects lend themselves to symmetrical arrangements and others to asymmetrical. Feng Shui principles insist that symmetry in rooms has a balancing effect. If you prefer symmetry as an organizing principle, group together pairs of lamps, candlesticks and lanterns, but vary their heights and shapes. Florists and display artists tend to take a very different approach to display, preferring to work with odd numbers rather than even. These asymmetrical compositions often find their own random logic and appear totally effortless.

English decorator David Hicks was fervent about displaying esoteric collections in the rooms he conceived.

OPPOSITE, BELOW RIGHT
A surreal narrative involving a crocodile and a cannon ball – like something straight out of *Alice in Wonderland.*

ABOVE LEFT Vintage prints and postcards can be matched to vintage frames.

ABOVE RIGHT A collection of wine-tasting tables forms an interesting backdrop to this garden.

ABOVE, CENTRE LEFT Empty frames artfully stacked on top of each other on a wooden table.

ABOVE, CENTRE RIGHT
A collection of biographies of film stars stacked on a side table.

BELOW RIGHT A child's pressed flower and insect collection on display in the kitchen.

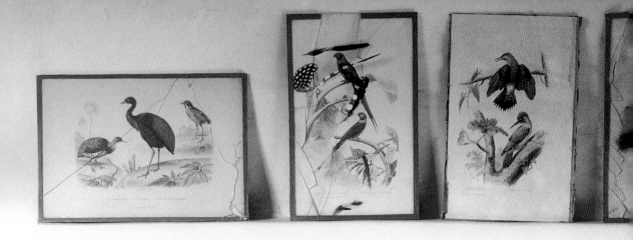

THIS PAGE Small prints always look better displayed *en masse*. Here a row of ornithological prints lean on a built-in ledge.

OPPOSITE, LEFT The quirky mixture of vintage finds suggests a corner in a favourite shop. A floral printed dress links visually with pink roses in an old glass decanter. The shop sign, child-sized mannequin and pile of cotton reels all conjure a romantic, shabby-chic atmosphere.

OPPOSITE, TOP RIGHT An Italian plaster figure, a scarlet rose in a glass bottle and chandelier drops conjure a feminine mood.

OPPOSITE, CENTRE RIGHT These elegant ceramics are not kept in a cupboard, but displayed on a buffet as a still life. Tactile balls of string, chosen for their texture and colour rather than any useful purpose, work with the neutrality of the setting.

OPPOSITE, BELOW RIGHT Even everyday objects can form interesting still lifes.

ABOVE LEFT A portrait of a 19th-century gentleman perches on top of a vellum suitcase.

ABOVE, CENTRE Card and paper filing drawers teamed with a vintage typewriter find an unlikely home at the end of a bed.

ABOVE RIGHT A clock without a face may no longer serve its original purpose, but its crumbling yet decorative gilt frame is still appreciated.

OPPOSITE (CLOCKWISE) The tarnished clockface echoes the eggshells' speckled surfaces. A wall clock with a decorative Chinoiserie case. An antique clockcase is used as a sculptural piece instead of a timepiece. A long stool used as a console is placed underneath a wall clock.

His famous 'tablescapes' were as artfully plotted as his grander decorating schemes. His formula involved selecting objects that were 'out of context', pointing out that the accessories you remember in somebody's house make their impact because they are 'unusual and unexpected'. He suggested that rather than dotting objects around a room they should be 'massed' together. He applied the same rule to pictures, particularly smaller ones. Paintings or photographs that share the same subject matter work best when hung together on one wall or simply in the same room, from groups of flower paintings and works depicting food to portraits.

Collections may also be useful. There is something deeply satisfying about an armoire stocked with beautifully laundered and folded linens. Linen fanatics delight in maintaining meticulous order, and such expert workmanship should not be hidden behind closed doors. A utility room, often treated as a storeroom for all that is habitually banished from sight, may also be aesthetically pleasing. Branded cleaning products in garish plastic containers can easily be decanted into labelled glass or ceramic bottles. Galvanized buckets, utilitarian wooden brushes and brooms, feather dusters, chamois leathers and Marseille soaps all have Shaker-like appeal for even the most reluctant housewife or cleaner. Collections hint at personal passions, the peculiar obsessions that enrich our lives, illustrating our connections with other cultures, nature and the world beyond the four walls of our homes.

The

Rooms

Kitchens & Dining Rooms

A FRENCH KITCHEN HAS A REPUTATION TO KEEP UP.
ARGUABLY THE MOST IMPORTANT SPACE IN THE HOME, IT
IS AN ENGINE ROOM, A ROOM FOR BOTH CREATIVITY AND
RELAXATION. THE WARMTH AND SENSUALITY OF A BUSY
KITCHEN MAKES IT THE MOST INVITING AND THEATRICAL
PLACE TO ENTERTAIN GUESTS AND THE MOST PRACTICAL
CENTRE FOR FAMILY LIFE. ONLY THE MOST SECRETIVE OR
INCOMPETENT COOK ENJOYS BEING ISOLATED FROM COMPANY.

THIS PAGE The highly decorative painted showcase with mirrored back is combined with a marble-topped *chocolatier's* table and simple rush-seated chairs in this rustic French dining room.

OPPOSITE, TOP LEFT The colour scheme may be monochromatic and the furniture utilitarian in this open-plan kitchen/dining room in southern France, but the look is composed and serene.

OPPOSITE, CENTRE AND RIGHT
Some items are typically French – a classic Duralex tumbler on a mirrored coaster, a dried gourd on an hexagonal plate and cheeses displayed on a weathered board.

As time spent at home is precious, multi-functional spaces have become more useful to 21st-century families than the traditional single-function room. We are more likely to spend time in a kitchen equipped with a generously proportioned table and comfortable chairs than in a room devoted solely to formal dining. In a small space, adding a café table and folding garden chairs makes the kitchen more social – somewhere to drink a *café crème* and read a newspaper.

Separate dining rooms, which often end up feeling rather lifeless and neglected, are rapidly becoming obsolete. If you are rethinking your living space, it may be possible to knock two reception rooms together to create a combined kitchen and dining room. For several decades, the familiar layout of a bourgeois domestic interior dedicated most space to a living room and considerably less to the kitchen, but many architects have recently reversed this idea, moving cooking and dining spaces into the largest rooms of a house.

Rows of slick, mass-produced fitted cupboards are unlikely to conjure a welcoming or authentic atmosphere (some state-of-the-art kitchens look more like laboratories than spaces devoted to the enjoyment of food). When the essentials are selected with a view to both form and function there is no need for the soulless uniformity of matching units. Instead opt for a simple, timeless solution such as a stand-alone range or Aga and a butler's sink stationed at a window, flanked by a work surface made from sturdy slabs of wood, slate or stone and fitted with shelves to house less aesthetically pleasing paraphernalia. Any clutter or pipes can be effectively hidden behind curtains made from utilitarian fabrics – antique linen sheets, striped mattress ticking or burlap. A free-standing piece of furniture, an

THIS PAGE, BOTTOM RIGHT
This austere dining room has been assembled from basic ingredients – café chairs and a wooden table with a linen runner.

ABOVE LEFT & RIGHT
This kitchen has been painted a warm grey and furnished with an antique cupboard and buffet and a large English table with a scrubbed wooden top teamed with a set of Swedish chairs. A pair of glass globe lights from a café are suspended over each end of the elongated table.

OPPOSITE, CLOCKWISE Open box shelving displays treasured objects. The only distraction from the pale colour scheme is a large atmospheric oil painting above the fireplace depicting a plate of grapes. The working end of the kitchen has been fitted with simply painted wooden units topped with limestone counters.

armoire or buffet can provide essential storage space for cutlery, tableware and provisions, as well as adding character to your kitchen.

Assemble an unfitted kitchen by picturing the space in the same way you would a living room, furnishing it with the same comforts. A chandelier hung above a kitchen table adds drama and contrasts with more rugged features, upholstered *fauteuil* chairs with arms invite guests to linger over the simplest meal, paintings hung on walls, and even a small sofa or armchair, all supply the character and softness required to balance the practical functions of the room. When it comes to lighting, dining

by candlelight in the evening enhances the atmosphere around the table, giving the scene an intimate, festive feel.

The passionate relationship between the French and their food is legendary. Their lifestyle is tailored to allow maximum enjoyment of every meal. Arrive in a French village or town between midday and 2PM, and you will find closed shops and deserted streets, but the restaurants and cafés will be buzzing with customers consuming all three courses of the *menu du jour*. Some employees even have the luxury of returning home to dine. By extension, the interior spaces devoted to the preparation and consumption of food

are designed, however artlessly, to be places to linger. A working fireplace or wood-burning stove is customary, particularly in the more rural areas of France.

Rather than hiding away the *batterie de cuisine* essential to the cook – pans, knives, pestle and mortar, pitchers and casserole dishes – the French are likely to display these close to hand on open shelves. These well-worn items, often made from natural materials such as terracotta, stoneware or wood, blend with their surroundings. They are the kitchen's classics, the perfect marriage of form and function, and add a touch of homeliness to any kitchen.

Cupboards in the French kitchen often have doors that are glazed or fitted with chicken wire so that the contents are visible. Compared with the 'fitted' kitchen, with all its opaque doors, this solution is eminently practical, rigged as it is to allow the cook easy access to ingredients. Herbs grow in terracotta pots on window-sills, baskets are laden with fruit and vegetables and *patisserie* is kept under glass cloches. The food becomes a part of the room, a visual feast.

Materials used in a French kitchen are not only chosen for their durability but also for their inherent style. Concrete is a flexible medium that is now widely used for floors and bespoke work surfaces, also incorporating shelves and cast sink units.

OPPOSITE There is a calculated austerity to this classic kitchen, which appears both well-organized and tranquil. The restrained colour scheme and utilitarian accessories add to the feeling of timelessness.

ABOVE LEFT A bunch of well-used wooden spoons are arranged like flowers in a square ceramic vase.

ABOVE RIGHT The uncluttered dining room (adjacent to the kitchen opposite) mixes painted furniture with a polished fruitwood table. A still life above the fireplace echoes the subtle shades employed in the room.

OPPOSITE, TOP A simple square table, slatted garden chairs, a shelf and a slim console are all that's needed to furnish this kitchen. It's the grey band of paint around the room that really holds the look together.

OPPOSITE, BELOW This timeless solution pulls together a shallow butler's sink, a butcher's block (used as a work surface) and simple linen curtains hiding pipes and clutter.

THIS PAGE, ABOVE An Aga, armchair and table fit into a space intended for a fire.

THIS PAGE, BELOW This 16th-century kitchen contains charming unfitted elements.

ABOVE LEFT A painting by François Sasmayoux adds contrast to the pale colour scheme.

ABOVE RIGHT A white linen cloth always looks effortlessly elegant set with silver flatware and white porcelain.

OPPOSITE The dramatic wirework chandelier and fireplace add a theatrical edge to an otherwise light and airy space.

For a stylish finish, it can be polished or coloured with pigment. Similarly muted in tone, limestone, slate, and wood are options that suit both period and modern architecture and also combine well with antiques. A kitchen isn't a kitchen without a sizeable multitasking table. This vital piece of furniture can be dressed up with laundered white linen for formal occasions or left scrubbed or waxed as a practical surface to prepare food and do homework.

Separate dining rooms, which are often left out of modern floor plans, have a more mannered and ceremonial air. They were conceived in the 18th century as a place to show off flatware, silver, porcelain, and fine linens, and their walls were hung with ancestral portraits and hunting trophies, the status symbols of another time. An element of this theatre is bound to endure, especially as dining is such a

THIS PAGE This dining room decorated in soft greys couldn't be simpler, but relies on architectural details, such as the elegant windows in the background for interest.

OPPOSITE, TOP LEFT Small tables pushed together create the effect of a long refectory table. Seating is provided by built-in banquettes and one long bench.

social activity. When we invite friends and family to dine with us at home, we want to show how *comme il faut* or how civilized we are. Setting a table with all the usual props may be something we do less in our fast-paced convenience-oriented age, but the desire to dine formally survives, especially in France where time is taken to enjoy every meal. Designing your kitchen with this in mind will allow you to create a comfortable and welcoming space, ideal for both everyday activities and formal dining.

ABOVE AND BELOW RIGHT
Simplicity is key to a French kitchen. Paella dishes sit on blue and white painted Valuris plates, ready for serving, and pomegranates add colour to the otherwise muted tones of the room.

THIS PAGE This contemporary kitchen design employs a monochrome colour scheme but mixes several textures to create interest. New materials, counter tops made from tinted polished concrete and glossy lacquered cabinets, contrast with rough stone walls and ancient wooden beams.

OPPOSITE (CLOCKWISE) The plainest low slung drum shades are suspended over the island. A low splashback provides a ledge on which to keep storage jars and decorative objects. Pale squash on a ceramic plate are the perfect accessories in this monochromatic colour scheme. A dish heaped with lemons adds vital colour.

Living Rooms

A LIVING ROOM ONLY DESERVES ITS NAME IF IT SUCCEEDS
IN FULFILLING MANY DIFFERENT FUNCTIONS. IF IT IS GOING
TO BE WORTH 'LIVING IN', TRULY USEFUL TO THE PEOPLE
IT ACCOMMODATES, IT SHOULD INCORPORATE SOMETHING
OF THEIR PERSONALITIES — AFTER ALL, IT IS ONE OF
THE HOME'S MOST PUBLIC ROOMS, THE PLACE WHERE
YOU DEFINE AND DISPLAY YOUR VALUES, YOUR HISTORY
AND YOUR TASTES TO GUESTS. IT IS ALSO LIKELY TO BE
THE LARGEST ROOM IN THE HOUSE — ALTHOUGH THIS IS
CHANGING, AND THE KITCHEN OF THE FUTURE MIGHT
SOON USURP ITS POSITION IN THE HIERARCHY. WHILE
THE 'HARDWARE' NECESSARY FOR THIS ROOM IS PROBABLY
LESS COSTLY THAN INSTALLING A NEW KITCHEN OR
BATHROOM, IT CAN BE TRICKY TO GET THE LOOK AND
FEEL RIGHT, ACHIEVING A BALANCE BETWEEN FORMALITY
AND INFORMALITY.

LEFT This 16th-century
farmhouse divides its living quarters
into distinct but connected spaces
(such as this library).

BELOW Sofas covered with
simple linen covers make this a
comfortable place for the family.

In the past, larger houses had at least two reception rooms – a formal drawing room and a more casual room for everyday use. The invention of loft-living revolutionized our ideas about communal spaces and the usual interior boundaries – walls and doors disappeared in favour of the multitasking living/dining/kitchen room. Some people simply prefer the intimacy of smaller separate rooms while others crave the adaptability of sociable open spaces.

A family is bound to use a living room for many different activities, so it will work better if it is divided into zones furnished for specific functions. These areas could include separate spaces to read, write, watch television, and relax with friends and family. However these are created, it's important that they are linked in style so that the feel of the room doesn't appear disjointed or uncomfortable.

OPPOSITE, BELOW RIGHT
An informal living room has been
decorated with a collection of
vintage floral textiles.

THIS PAGE Tobit Roche's canvas
gives this room a meditative
atmosphere and a burst of colour.

The fireplace is still an iconic, desirable fixture in many homes despite efficient modern heating options. Nothing can replace it. We continue to attach enormous importance to the element of fire. Who can resist its sensual spell – the hypnotic effect of flickering flames, the scent of wood burning and the accompanying crackle and hiss? An open fire or stove promotes a feeling of deep relaxation and calm, so naturally a living room benefits from having a chimney piece or wood-burning stove as a focal point. Sofas and chairs will inevitably end up positioned near the fire to be closer to its comforting warmth. During summer months empty hearths can be dressed with silver birch logs or fresh boughs of pine.

The first truly comfortable chair – the *bergère* – was invented in France in the 18th century. An upholstered, overstuffed armchair with an exposed wood frame, wide proportions and a loose seat cushion, this style of chair represented a comfortable alternative to its stalwart predecessors. Before this, chairs were straight-backed, hard, and designed to confer status on the sitter rather than to provide comfort and repose. From the reign of Louis XV onwards, grand houses distinguished between two types of furniture – *sièges meublants* (formal chairs that were ranged in a line against the *boiseries*) and *sièges courants* (portable chairs that were light enough to be moved around to wherever the most enticing conversation or card game was taking place). Another example of this style of chair is a *voyeuse*, a version of a *siège courant* designed to be sat on back-to-front, with one's arms resting on the back.

Perhaps as a result of this sophisticated variety in the shape and style of seating in a salon, the French are unlikely to furnish a living room with a matching suite. Two sofas, differing in shape and style but upholstered in similar or identical fabric, combined with diverse chairs and an ottoman or low table, are a more apt and imaginative mélange. Indeed the mix of pieces is the key to whether the room is

OPPOSITE A contemporary sofa is positioned around a large coffee table fashioned from an old door. A painting by New Zealand artist John Crawford hangs above.

THIS PAGE A wood-burning stove suits the sparse architecture of this old *bergerie*. The wheelbarrow is the ultimate utilitarian log basket.

OPPOSITE The built-in seating, tiled floor and decorative border in this attic space give it a Moorish feel. The one decorative extravagance is the customized chandelier.

THIS PAGE This painted console, teamed with a carved marble mirror and lamp, houses a row of useful storage baskets, ideal for containing clutter.

successful both visually and physically. It's still acceptable to furnish a room with some *sièges courants*. They add flexibility essential in a space devoted to entertaining visitors. You will often find that 18th- and 19th-century French salon chairs are sold in pairs, allowing you to bring an element of symmetry to the arrangement of a room.

Fitted carpet is as redundant in the French salon as the three-piece suite. Wooden parquet, terracotta, stone or marble floors may sport rugs, and these are often regarded as a decorative texture, essential to the look and feel of the room. In southern France the coolness of ceramic, marble and stone floors make them a traditional practical choice. When warmth underfoot is required, kilims, Aubussons and bound sisal rugs and runners are used as alternatives to carpet. As most French

OPPOSITE, TOP LEFT A pair of Scandinavian caramel leather chairs give a contemporary edge to a relaxed living space.

OPPOSITE, BELOW LEFT An aerial view of the chateau and grounds leans on the mantelpiece of the stone fire surround.

CENTRE The vintage child's racing car sitting on the Indian coffee table is appreciated as a sculptural object as well as a toy.

THIS PAGE, TOP RIGHT An eclectic combination of streamlined 1960s sideboard sitting next to a 19th-century velvet upholstered buttoned armchair and accessorized with a lamp base carved in the form of a classical urn.

THIS PAGE, BELOW RIGHT A large framed map of France hangs above a classic English George Smith sofa in a neutral colour scheme.

homes are fitted with internal and external shutters, thick, blackout curtains are not strictly necessary. Accordingly window treatments are less structured and some windows, particularly those with interesting architectural frames or glazed doors, go bare. A stylish combination of French period style mixed with modern-day chic will help bring your living room together.

THIS PAGE In the corner of this room, rectilinear tables are combined with a curvaceous reproduction *fauteuil* and accessorized with African sculptures and a pile of antique leather-bound books. In another part of the room, white anemones contrast with the stark black of the *fauteuils*.

OPPOSITE Modern blends stylishly with ancient in this living space. Reclaimed balustrades have been used for the mezzanine level library area.

LEFT, TOP RIGHT, BOTTOM
RIGHT The architecture of the
reception room in a 16th-century
house provides plenty of textures
for a space that is cosy, but avoids
cottage clichés, furnished with a
mixture of mid-century pieces,
two identical Ikea sofas and a
woven goat hair rug.

Bedrooms

THE BEDROOM IS UNIVERSALLY REGARDED AS THE MOST
PERSONAL ROOM IN THE HOME. THOSE WHO SIMPLY
REQUIRE A FUNCTIONAL SPACE IN WHICH TO SLEEP AND
DRESS ARE LIKELY TO DECORATE THEIR INNER SANCTUM
WITH RESTRAINT, CONCENTRATING ON THE QUALITY OF
COMFORTS THE ROOM PROVIDES — LUXURIOUS SHEETS,
AMPLE STORAGE, APPROPRIATE LIGHTING, THE ELEMENTS
THAT ENSURE A RESTFUL EXPERIENCE. OTHERS, MORE
INCLINED TO REGARD THE BEDROOM AS A DEN, A PLACE
TO LUXURIATE IN, EXPLOIT THE OPPORTUNITY FOR SELF-
EXPRESSION. THE FRENCH WORD BOUDOIR USUALLY
CONJURES UP THE NOTION OF AN INDULGENT FEMININE
RETREAT — A LUXURIOUSLY APPOINTED MAGPIE'S NEST
OF PERSONAL TREASURES, A HAVEN FILLED WITH ALL
MANNER OF FRIVOLOUS FRIPPERIES AND A REPOSITORY
FOR A DELICIOUS ARMOURY OF LOTIONS, JEWELS AND
DECORATIVE TRIFLES.

THIS PAGE Bedrooms do not need to be elaborately furnished. Comfort and a feeling of serenity are the most vital ingredients. This pared-down bedroom has only bare essentials, but a floral trellis-pattern wallpaper, an atmospheric oil painting of an angel and meticulously laundered linens ensure a tranquil mood.

The verb *bouder* literally translates as 'to sulk' and suggests how the concept encompasses much more than a dormitory – it is a place to re-create oneself, daydream, to receive visitors, and linger in solitary splendour on a sofa or chaise longue eating bonbons.

A 17th-century invention, the boudoir evolved as a reaction to the public nature of the *Levée* (the Grand Awakening ceremony instigated by Louis XIV). The Marquise de Rambouillet, hostess of the infamous Hôtel de Rambouillet (a renowned literary salon) and trendsetter in domestic interiors at the time, was flattered when King Louis XIII and Queen Anne followed her example and installed an *appartement* of smaller, cosier rooms at Versailles. It included a boudoir where the queen could withdraw from the glare of court life and spend time alone or with more intimate companions. The decorative style of this new space became more exuberantly personal than the style of other rooms in the house. At the chateau of Fontainebleau, the queen's quarters boast silver walls painted with arabesques, mirrors and gold leaf and a gilded desk inlaid with mother-of-pearl.

Until the 19th century the bedroom was a reception room. Once the curtains around the bed were drawn, the room might be used for entertaining, bathing and even eating. The bed was undoubtedly the most important piece of furniture in the house – and perhaps the most expensive. At Versailles, the *Levée* was a pivotal part of court pageantry. The theatrical ritual required the royal entourage to pay homage as the king or queen dressed, bathed and got in or out of bed, and, because it was such a formal occasion, it required a suitably grand and exquisitely embellished bed placed on a dais to allow maximum visibility.

The rococo period emerged in France in the early 18th century and was marked by highly decorative and lavish styling; walls painted with nymphs and cherubs, carved and gilded mirrors, lustrous silk upholstery, lace trimmings and beds adorned

OPPOSITE In a minimal space, touches of silver conjure a feeling of high opulence, a contrast with the chalky stone. Red anemones add a refreshing burst of primary colour.

ABOVE A shimmering silver gilt wall behind the divan bed 'mirrors' the silvered chairs, mirror frame and table opposite. The laser-cut metal garland (by Tord Boontje) hung from a wall bracket, conceals a light bulb.

with canopies and curtains suspended from a corona. Such indulgence does not necessarily prescribe a bedroom in the contemporary French style, but elements from the boudoir concept have survived and flourished (note the current vogue for rampantly feminine styling – chinoiserie wallpapers, lavish silk or velvet quilts, laces and voiles and coquettish little dressing tables). Today the idea that the inner sanctum of our home might more readily express who we are than the 'public' rooms is plainly just as relevant as it was in the 18th century, however spare or understated the room and its furnishings.

A room made for sleeping in requires muted colours rather than stimulating ones and functional pieces of furniture – somewhere to keep a lamp and a book, very little clutter, storage for clothes, and few distractions from the business of relaxation. Most bedroom schemes, even the most accidental, probably start with the bed and its position in a room. Sometimes the linens that dress it are more pivotal to the 'look' than other elements. The most straightforward option is a divan bed, which can be layered with the crispest sheets for summer and made cosier in winter with quilts, blankets, eiderdowns and throws that may add flashes of colour. Even the most monastic *chambre à coucher* can be made more sensually inviting by playing with textures. When seasons change, alternating these textiles is the

ABOVE A 'foxed' section of mirror leans against a wall reflecting the daisies in the bottles.

OPPOSITE, TOP LEFT
The composed atmosphere of this bedroom has been achieved by painting walls and all architectural details white. Carefully chosen objects, glass and textiles seem to float in space.

OPPOSITE, BELOW LEFT
A palette of taupe, silver and white is a good neutral alternative to white. Brighter accent colours, like the pink of the anemones on the table, can be added in small doses.

OPPOSITE, RIGHT Adding an antique corona with ethereal muslin drapes suits the architecture and customizes this simple bed.

quickest and simplest way to transform the atmosphere of the bedroom. The French
are less inclined to use down-filled duvets preferring a combination of sheets and
quilts or *boutis*, plus large 60-cm-square pillows with a long bolster underneath.

Elaborate bed frames lend instant character to a room. A bed *à la Polonaise*,
with its tall framework, lends an architectural edge to an otherwise sparsely
furnished room. Originally this style was popular because it sported draught-
excluding drapes, which provided added warmth during a period without central
heating. Alcove beds, hidden behind curtains, were another cosy option. Most
antique beds are comprised of a carved, caned or upholstered head and footboard
held together by two side sections. Sometimes the headboard is used alone and
teamed with a divan. The *lit bateau* (an Empire-style bed with more masculine

lines), on the other hand, is habitually made of a dark wood such as mahogany or rosewood, and has classical curved ends based on the prow of a boat. Creative alternatives to the traditional headboard include decorative doors or screens, textiles, or even a plaster panel. These can make a refreshing and interesting change to standard designs, as well as adding textural variety to a room.

Anyone who has travelled in France will certainly have noticed the penchant for using fabric on walls. *Toile de Jouy* from top to bottom is not an uncommon look for a bedroom.

OPPOSITE A floral *boutis* with a black background balances the dark monochrome prints. A classic café table is used indoors.

ABOVE LEFT The *azulejos* and ochre pigment standing in for a headboard give this bedroom a Southern Mediterranean flavour.

ABOVE RIGHT A *lit bateau* fastidiously made up in plain white linens makes this traditional room a soothing space to relax in.

The material is usually stretched and nailed to a wooden framework, and is often repeated on bedcovers and curtains. The effect is indelibly Gallic, and rather like sleeping in a chic tent. Fabric walls cannot help but look very 'finished', smart and indulgent. As many French homes have shutters, fabric window treatments tend to be simple and unstructured (the monogrammed antique wedding sheet often doubles as curtains), a far cry from the lined and interlined, elaborately headed type favoured elsewhere.

Whether you use your bedroom as a boudoir (with all its sociable implications) or *chambre à coucher* (a place to retreat to), the keynote for your scheme should be comfort.

OPPOSITE, TOP LEFT
The florist's bucket filled with a tangle of red blooms breaks the austerity of the room.

OPPOSITE, BELOW LEFT
Warm grey walls, white linen, dark beams and hunting trophies conjure a rustic unfussy look.

OPPOSITE, BELOW RIGHT
Natural colours and materials create an unpretentious French country bedroom.

ABOVE The deep red oxide band of paint defines the furnished area. The dash of red in the floral lampshades unites the elements of the room and an area of pebbled floor adds outdoor texture.

OPPOSITE AND TOP LEFT The Elizabethan-influenced black-and-white fresco secco is painted directly onto the walls making a decorative background for a simple bed. The glass and metal lamp and the purple flowers on the bedside table form an elegant contrast to the patterned wall.

ABOVE RIGHT A mid-century chair, reminiscent of country pieces designed decades before.

LEFT The walnut chest of drawers has markings that echo the decorative pattern of the frescoed walls.

Bathrooms

THE BATHROOM IS OFTEN A WELCOME SANCTUARY FROM
MORE PUBLIC ROOMS IN YOUR HOME; SOMEWHERE WHERE
YOU CAN LEGITIMATELY SPEND TIME ALONE BEHIND A
LOCKED DOOR. ALTHOUGH WE ARE ACCUSTOMED TO GIVING
OUR BATHROOMS A CLINICAL LOOK, WITH TILED WALLS AND
FLOORS AND UTILITARIAN ACCESSORIES, THIS IS LARGELY
UNNECESSARY. BATHROOMS MAKE A WONDERFUL PLACE TO
READ, LISTEN TO THE RADIO OR MUSIC OR MEDITATE, SO
ADD AN ARMCHAIR OR SMALL SOFA IF THE SPACE ALLOWS.
IF YOU HAVE A WINDOW, ORIENT THE BATH SO THAT
YOU CAN CONTEMPLATE THE VIEW WHILE YOU BATHE.

ABOVE LEFT AND RIGHT
A long stone trough set on wooden legs is a smart alternative to a porcelain basin. In this streamlined design, nickel taps have been set into the back of the stone trough and a large silver-framed mirror leans on the ledge.

OPPOSITE With its vaulted ceiling, arched alcoves and innovative stone bath, this room is more spa than *salle de bains*.

An increased interest in the benefits of 'well-being products' laced with essential oils and healing unguents has initiated a new attitude to the bathroom. We are more inclined to think of it as a spa rather than as a sanitation station. This shift has encouraged us to consider other ways of configuring and decorating the room. It is not uncommon to sacrifice a spare bedroom in order to make a larger-than-average indulgent bathroom or to incorporate a bath into a bedroom. In this *mise en scène*, the bathtub becomes somewhere to unwind and renew ourselves, a sensual and transforming experience instead of a dutiful, mechanical one. Perhaps Cornell University professor Alexander Kira was heading in the right direction when his study of the bathroom concluded that it has 'living-room potential'. With most of us living such fast-paced lifestyles, we long for a private place to unwind.

ABOVE The painting of a chic woman in 1950s dress above the reproduction Napoleonic-style free-standing bath strikes an elegant note and personalizes a room that otherwise might feel masculine.

OPPOSITE An elegant reproduction porcelain basin combined with a 19th-century overmantel mirror. The addition of an unusual rattan and velvet shell-shaped chair lends softness to the room.

In France a bathroom is likely to incorporate antiques and to try harder to resemble a normal room (rather than a sterile hospital-in-the-home). The space-saving suite is superseded by unmatched elements – a wooden or metal washstand with a plumbed-in sink instead of a bowl, a free-standing tub or steel bath panelled with wood, stone or marble, and a bidet. This flexible, mix-and-match arrangement is probably a hangover from the days before plumbing when a tub was portable and a bowl and jug stood in for a wash basin with taps. Colours and materials used tend to be natural – limestone, terracotta, slate, watery shades of blue and green – emphasizing the connection between a room used for relaxing in water and the beach. You won't find sets of matching towel rail, cabinet, shelf, etc. in *la salle de bains*; a vintage ladder leaning against a wall, a chest of drawers or table, a basket, and a decorative mirror serve these purposes beautifully and effectively. The ever-useful antique linen sheet softens the look, as a curtain at a window or screening-off plumbing and clutter under a sink.

Larger bathrooms in France will often be furnished with a cupboard or linen press to store towels and lotions and potions. Still lifes of shells and pebbles or flowers and glass vessels help personalize an area that is traditionally less accessorized than other rooms in the home. Oil paintings can be affected by humidity, but any art displayed behind glass should be safe and will add texture and colour. If you want to avoid tiles, paint walls with eggshell or gloss paint or, alternatively, you can seal raw plaster with wax. For an added piece of luxury, you can also introduce underfloor heating to a room fitted with a cool stone or tile floor.

Recently designers have re-evaluated the shapes and materials used for sanitary ware. The white porcelain pedestal basin is rather out of favour in state-of-the-art bathrooms. Modern basins are more likely to resemble a bowl, sitting on top

of a bench or table. Elongated, trough-like sinks made of stone slabs (reminiscent of agricultural drinking troughs) are teamed with sleek, ingeniously constructed stone baths. Cedarwood, which does not rot, is a tactile alternative to tiles or stone and may be used for floors, walls and even sinks and baths. Minimalist architect Claudio Silvestrin has even furnished bathrooms with deep wooden baths that give the space a tranquil and natural atmosphere.

The recycled bathroom, a combination of reclaimed elements, works well in a period house. These basics can be found in junk and antique shops, as well as in salvage yards. You'll find that most vintage and antique sanitary ware can be reconditioned by expert restoration companies. Cast-iron baths can be re-enamelled, but reproduction versions are also easy to find and you have the added option of

being able to have the outer side painted to suit your colour scheme. If you don't want a free-standing bath or if your room is too small to accommodate one, choose one that can be 'boxed in'. An accomplished carpenter can hide pipes and cisterns behind panels, giving the room a streamlined, contemporary look. Alternatively, you can hide any visible clutter behind a strategically placed curtain.

As you design your bathroom, don't be afraid to approach it as a real room, combining interesting textures with unexpected comforts. Temper practicality (waterproof surfaces and efficient plumbing) with a creative approach to accessories. Paintings, sculptures, candlesticks, flowers and plants add character and sophistication to a space that is often impersonal and cold. The smaller details of your bathroom are just as important as the overall scheme.

OPPOSITE, TOP LEFT
A butler's sink, reclaimed taps and wooden draining board suggest old-world charm in a utility room.

OPPOSITE, TOP RIGHT
This painted trunk artfully hides bathroom clutter.

OPPOSITE, BELOW LEFT
The platform for this bath provides the perfect view.

ABOVE LEFT The ageless charm of this free-standing bath is enhanced by the intriguing period paintings displayed above.

ABOVE RIGHT A characterful combination of a gnarled marble sink set into a vanity unit decorated with blue and white tiles.

OPPOSITE, TOP LEFT An updated version of washstand and bowl where round porcelain sinks sit on top of the built-in vanity unit. Walls are finished with tongue-and-groove panels and hung with antique mirrors, giving the room a pretty country feel.

OPPOSITE, BELOW LEFT In a simply decorated attic bathroom the crepuscular oil painting and ancient floorboards balance paler colours.

OPPOSITE, RIGHT A white wood-panelled wall gives this simple white bathroom a soft, natural mood.

ABOVE LEFT The black tiling and polished tinted concrete give this wet room a chic, graphic look.

ABOVE RIGHT A stone torso of Venus mounted on a plinth acts as a visual link to the stone used to divide the wet room from the area housing sink and toilet.

Workrooms

A WORKROOM NEED NOT IMITATE THE BLANDNESS OF
THE TRADITIONAL OFFICE SPACE, BUT WE ARE PROBABLY AT
OUR MOST CREATIVE IN A PLACE THAT PROMOTES A SENSE
OF ORDER AND CALM. THE ARRIVAL OF THE COMPUTER,
INTERNET AND OTHER ELECTRONIC WIZARDRY HAVE MADE
IT POSSIBLE FOR MANY OF US TO WORK FROM HOME,
MAKING THE STUDY OR WORKROOM A DESIRABLE BUT
PROBLEMATIC SPACE, BUT AN AMENITY THAT WE NEED TO
FIND ROOM FOR NONETHELESS. HOW DO WE ASSIMILATE
THIS ROOM VISUALLY AND PHYSICALLY INTO A DOMESTIC
INTERIOR? AND WHERE DO WE DRAW THE LINE BETWEEN
WORK AND PLAY?

THIS PAGE This neat little secretaire desk fits discreetly into a bedroom. Its hinged work surface opens to reveal useful storage compartments.

OPPOSITE A serving table with a vellum top is put into service here as a long, narrow desk. The strip of wall above the desk is the ideal place to hang smaller pictures and mirrors, as well as a decorative plaque from the owner's university college.

The versatile living and workspace favoured by artists, artisans, photographers and other freelancers might seem relatively new to us, but in the past most work was based in or around the home. The upper classes prized their libraries, and many craftsmen had workshops attached to or next to their homes. Then at some point during the 19th century, working from home was no longer considered 'proper' for the bourgeoisie and centralized workplaces became the norm.

Working from home has many obvious advantages, but the requisite office hardware with all its wires and appendages can seem alien, especially in a space filled with natural textures and carefully chosen antiques. The wireless laptop, the model of sleek, discreet design, can be moved around easily, and armoires,

sideboards, and vintage shop display units can be adapted as ideal alternatives to secretaries, filing cabinets and other traditional storage solutions. A draper's cabinet, with its many drawers, can compartmentalize all manner of reference material and paperwork. Any capacious free-standing cupboard may be adapted to house an entire office – fitted with shelves to house box files and even a shelf that extends or folds out to form a neat desk.

Interior and fashion designers always use oversized pin boards when they are researching new collections, and the resulting collage is often a work of art in itself. Assemble and display the things that inspire you most on the wall nearest to your desk – a collage of inspirational images, postcards, magazine tear sheets,

OPPOSITE A tall painted vitrine provides an ideal storage place for books.

BELOW RIGHT In a versatile space, devoted to both work and play, reclaimed panels are adapted to form fitted cupboards.

BELOW LEFT An 18th-century demi-lune table is used as a work table when teamed with this distressed leather chair.

collections of *objets trouvés*, paintings, or an extravagantly framed blackboard or cork pin board for messages and lists.

If you can't devote a whole room to work, designate a 'zone' within an existing room, but make sure the furniture blends with the colour palette and overall look and feel of the room. Bespoke built-in shelves are a good solution in awkward spaces, attics or alcoves. Most houses and apartments have a small box room or underused space on a landing or tucked under a staircase that, with some ingenuity, can be put to use as an office or workspace. Then all you need to add is a comfortable chair and directional lighting from an anglepoise lamp.

Recently the designer shed, a well-appointed outdoor room, has come into its own as the solution for expanding families who have outgrown their homes or for people who prefer to separate their domestic scene from their workplace.

ABOVE LEFT A fireplace effectively and neatly frames this work area in a bedroom.

ABOVE CENTRE An elongated narrow table pressed into a corner and surrounded by a settle and a chaise longue comprises an area the owner uses as a 'workshop' for creating innovative lighting.

ABOVE RIGHT A piano assimilated into the room as both console table and instrument, is elegantly framed with pictures and a quirky lamp.

OPPOSITE An oak dining table stationed opposite an abstract painting by Tobit Roche doubles as a desk, spacious enough to stack with piles of reference books and with ample room to spread out any work.

Outdoor Spaces

THE FRENCH APPLY THE SAME SUBTLETY AND SOPHISTICATION
TO OUTDOOR SPACES AS THEY DO TO THE INTERIORS OF
THEIR HOMES. GARDENS, BALCONIES AND TERRACES ARE
TREATED AS AN EXTENSION OF THE INTERIOR AND
FURNISHED ACCORDINGLY WITH FURNITURE, TEXTILES
AND OTHER PIECES ORIGINALLY DESIGNED TO BE USED
INSIDE, SUCH AS FOLDING METAL CAMPAIGN BEDS. AN
OLD KITCHEN TABLE WITH A FLAKING PAINTED BASE AND
BLEACHED WEATHER-BEATEN TOP WOULD NOT LOOK OUT
OF PLACE IN A FRENCH GARDEN. THE PATINA OF AGE —
LAYERS OF PEELING PAINT ON WOOD AND METAL, LICHEN
ON STONE AND CANVAS FADED BY EXPOSURE TO THE SUN —
IS ALL PART OF THE LOOK.

THIS PAGE The discreet doors to French country houses and their gardens or courtyards are often made from oak and held together with hand-forged studs. Colours tend to be muted greys that blend with the stone or pigment-washed walls of the buildings. The linen sheet (centre, right) is employed as a make-shift door to an outside space.

OPPOSITE An ancient stone font outside a house in the south of France looks at home set against this roughly plastered wall.

If the French have a knack for selecting furnishings that seem to have been in the family for years, it may be because they have, but it may also be that the taste for old, often imperfect things is hardwired into their collective subconscious. Bargain-basement moulded plastic chairs, and Day-Glo melamine tableware are too garish, too synthetic, and too kitsch to merit space in the French garden.

Parisian parks have always been elegantly conceived. The Jardin du Luxembourg and the Jardin des Tuileries are generously equipped with those iconic little slatted metal chairs painted the darkest green or a soft verdigris. The darker green blends perfectly with the manicured but natural setting and is used for pavilions, kiosks and other structures because it renders them almost invisible. Underfoot, you won't find tarmac but wide avenues packed with gritty compacted sand known by landscape architects and gardeners as 'Paris dust'. In daylight (and even at dusk) its whiteness shimmers and endless vistas take on a magical haze. After strolling through the park, your shoes will be covered in chalky residue, but there is something undeniably glamorous about walking on a carpet of Paris dust!

Outdoor spaces can make idyllic places to dine. In the south of France, the garden or courtyard is treated as a cooler dining room and is presented as such, with tables covered with linen cloths and laid with glasses and cutlery and seats

OPPOSITE An apple tree provides a shady spot for a swing created from an old bench.

ABOVE LEFT An outdoor storage space is both aesthetically pleasing and practical. A shelf laden with empty wine bottles is fixed to the stone wall above large glazed Andouzes pots ready to be planted.

ABOVE, CENTRE Many things find a new, decorative purpose in a French garden, even if they are in a state of decay. This original mobile was assembled from objects found with a metal detector.

ABOVE RIGHT A birdcage entwined with leaves becomes a natural part of the garden.

ABOVE LEFT The utilitarian basics; a painted wooden table and weathered slatted chairs merge with the soft shades of the southern French landscape.

ABOVE RIGHT A row of rusty horseshoes find a home on a red-brick ledge.

RIGHT The iconic French Renault 4 looks at home in the landscape.

OPPOSITE A weather-beaten wooden chair becomes a part of nature set against the rough bark of an ancient olive tree.

LEFT This kitchen table's weathered surface is covered with a collection of terracotta roof finials that blend tonally with its distressed paint.

BELOW The colours of the South; pale terracotta pigment for walls (also highlighted in the roses) and a greyish blue for woodwork.

OPPOSITE A metal campaign bed in an internal courtyard has been dressed with vintage textiles.

made comfortable with cushions. In clement weather, other areas of the garden will be transformed into temporary living areas furnished with awnings, hammocks, parasols, rugs, and daybeds strewn with pillows and quilts. Even mirrors find their way into a natural setting, effectively magnifying space and offering window-like views.

The muted colours of box and olive trees, lavenders and sage plants make them essential choices for all types of French garden. Plants are displayed in classically shaped terracotta pots and stone or cast-iron urns. Hard landscaping, which gives the more formal garden its structure, is built with sections of new or ancient stone and paths are laid with stone sets, shingle or terracotta tiles. Seventeenth-century gardens, like the Jardin du Luxembourg, were laid out geometrically with boxwood parterres in gravel beds. The philosophy behind this formality was concerned with man's ability to exert control over nature, but the 18th century brought a freer style with winding paths and an untamed look popularized by British garden designers Capability Brown and Humphry Repton. Marie Antoinette's garden at the Petit Trianon was cultivated in this looser style of gardening. You will still find both approaches represented in France today, both in rural and urban landscapes.

SOURCE DIRECTORY

ANTIQUES

Josephine Ryan Antiques
www.josephineryan
antiques.co.uk
Chandeliers, antique mirrors, furniture and accessories.

Ann-Morris Antiques
239 East 60th Street
New York, NY 10022
212 755 3308
Antique furniture, lamps and accessories.

Appley Hoare
www.appleyhoare.com
020 7351 5206
French country antiques.

Bazar
82 Golborne Road
London W10 5PS
020 8969 6262
French decorative antiques.

Chez Zoe
www.chezzoe.net
Decorative antiques sold online from a captain's cabin in Sagaponack, NY.

Elizabeth Street Gallery
209 Elizabeth Street
New York, NY 10012
www.elizabethstreetgallery.com
212 941 4800
Architectural antiques, furniture and stonework.

Eron Johnson Antiques, Ltd.
389 South Lipan Street
Denver, CO 80223
303 777 8700
www.eronjohnsonantiques.com
Online retailer of antique table lamps, wall sconces, candelabra, chandeliers and more.

The French House
41–43 Parsons Green Lane
London SW6 4HH
020 7371 7573
www.thefrenchhouse.co.uk
Antiques, fabrics and upholstery.

Relic Antiques
Malcolm Gliksten
133–135 Pancras Road
London NW1 1UN
020 7485 7810
Fairground art and antiques.

Robert Young Antiques
68 Battersea Bridge Road
London SW11 3AG
020 7228 7847
www.robertyoungantiques.com
Country and provincial antiques.

Petworth, West Sussex
www.paada.com
Petworth in West Sussex is known for its antique shops.

Tetbury, Gloucestershire
www.tetburyonline.co.uk
This Gloucestershire town has a huge selection of antique shops.

SALVAGE & RECLAMATION

Architectural Accents
2711 Piedmont Road NE
Atlanta, GA 30305
404 266 8700
www.architecturalaccents.com
Reproduction stone mantels in the French style.

Andy Thornton Architectural Antiques Ltd.
Victoria Mills
Stainland Road
Greetland
Halifax
West Yorkshire HX4 8AD
01422 376000
www.andythornton.com
Architectural antiques.

Lassco
30 Wandsworth Road
London SW8 2LG
020 7394 2100
www.lassco.co.uk
Architectural antiques, salvaged floors, doors, sanitaryware etc.

TEXTILES & WALLPAPERS

Cabbages and Roses
www.cabbagesandroses.com
Nostalgic wallpapers and fabrics.

Cole & Son (Wallpapers) Ltd.
www.cole-and-son.com
Manufacturers of fine printed wallpapers.

Gracious Home
1220 3rd Avenue
New York, NY 10021
212 517 6300
www.gracioushome.com
Bedding, linens, fine fixtures, and other home accessories.

Jane Sacchi Linens
134 Lots Road
London SW10 0RJ
Antique linen and accessories.

Katharine Pole
www.katharinepole.com
Upholstered furniture and rustic linens.

Thibaut
800 223 0704
www.thibautdesign.com
Textiles and wallpaper.

Whaleys (Bradford) Ltd
www.whaleys-bradford.ltd.uk
Utility fabrics.

FURNITURE & ACCESSORIES

Astier de Villatte
www.astierdevillatte.com
Elegant and simple faïence china.

Crate & Barrel
www.crateandbarrel.com
French-style pieces, including marble-topped tables and classic bistro-style bentwood chairs.

La Maison
107–108 Shoreditch High St
London E1 6JN
020 7729 9646
www.atlamaison.com
Great selection of beds.

PAINTS, TILES & FLOORING

Country Floors
www.countryfloors.com
Ceramics, stone and terracotta in the country style.

Farrow & Ball
www.farrow-ball.com
Paint in subtle, muted shades.

Old Fashioned Milk Paint Company
www.milkpaint.com
Paints from natural pigments.

The Paint and Paper Library
3 Elystan Street
London SW3 3NT
020 7823 7755
www.paintlibrary.co.uk
Paint and wallpapers.

Papers and Paints
4 Park Walk
London SW10 0AD
020 7352 8626
www.papers-paints.co.uk
Historical and traditional colours.

Paris Ceramics
www.parisceramics.com
Limestone, terracotta, antique stone and hand-painted tiles.

KITCHENS

Forneaux de France
www.lacanche.co.uk
Makers of Lacanche and Fornair range-style cookers.

The French House
www.thefrenchhouse.net
Copper pans, earthenware, copper sinks, pure linen tea towels and ceramic lights.

IKEA
www.ikea.com
Reasonably priced kitchens.

BATHROOMS

Catchpole & Rye
Saracens Dairy
Pluckley Lane
Pluckley
Kent TN27 0SA
01233 840840
www.catchpoleandrye.com
Antique and reproduction sanitaryware.

Restoration Hardware
935 Broadway
New York, NY 10010-6009
212 260 9479
www.restorationhardware.com
Bathroom furniture based on classic French cabinetry.

Stiffkey Bathrooms
89 Upper St Giles Street
Norwich NR2 1AB
01603 627850
www.stiffkeybathrooms.com
Antique sanitaryware and their own range of period and bespoke bathroom accessories.

LIGHTING

David Canepa Lighting
www.canepalighting.co.uk
Pretty, gilded wall lights and chandeliers.

MIRRORS

Jasper Jacks
www.jasperjacks.com
Antique French mirrors.

GARDEN FURNITURE & ORNAMENTS

1Hundred
07782 233 9699
www.1hundred.co
18th-, 19th- and 20th-century garden ornament, as well as furniture and decorative items.

Detroit Garden Works
1794 Pontiac Drive
Sylvan Lake, MI 48320
248 335 8089
www.detroitgardenworks.com
French and English garden antiques and landscaping.

FAIRS & MARKETS

UK

Adam's Antiques fair
The Royal Horticultural Hall
Lindley Hall, Elverton Street
London SW1P 2PE
www.adamsantiquesfairs.com
A monthly event for antiques dealers. Check website for dates.

The Decorative Antiques and Textiles Fair
www.decorativefair.com
London
An excellent source of high-quality, competitively priced antiques and 20th-century design.

FRANCE

L'Isle-sur-la-Sorgue
A historic town famous for its antique shops.

Puces de Saint-Ouen
Flea market situated at Portes de Clignancourt, Paris. Open Saturdays, Sundays and Mondays from 10am–1pm and 2pm–5.30pm. Genuine bric-à-brac with more than 300 antique dealers.

US

Hell's Kitchen Flea Market
West 39th Street
New York, NY
212 243 5343
www.hellskitchenfleamarket.com
Every Saturday and Sunday, 9am–5pm.

Brimfield Antique Show
Route 20
Brimfield, MA 01010
www.brimfieldshow.com
This famous flea market runs for a week in May, July, and September.

Georgetown Flea Market
1819 35th Street NW
Washington, D.C.
202 775 FLEA
www.georgetownfleamarket.com
Open Sundays.

Flea Markets Across America
www.fleamarketsacross
america.com
Useful listings of flea markets across the country.

PICTURE CREDITS

ALL PHOTOGRAPHY BY CLAIRE RICHARDSON.
KEY: a=above, b=below, r=right, l=left, c=centre

Endpapers Josephine Ryan Antiques, www.josephineryanantiques.co.uk;
1 Josephine Ryan Antiques, www.josephineryanantiques.co.uk; 2–3
www.les-sardines.com; 4 l The Home of Charmaine & Paul Jack – Belvezet,
France; 4 r The home of Fiona and Woody Woodhouse in Herefordshire; 5
Harriet Anstruther's home in Sussex; 6 www.chambres-provence.com; 8–10
all Josephine Ryan Antiques, www.josephineryanantiques.co.uk; except 10 br
Malcolm Gliksten's home in France; 11 Josephine Ryan Antiques,
www.josephineryanantiques.co.uk; 14 The home of Fiona and Woody Woodhouse
in Herefordshire; 16 al & ar The home of Fiona and Woody Woodhouse in
Herefordshire; 16 acl Les Trois Salons, Uzès – Creators and owners Charmaine
& Paul Jack; 16 acr Nick & Flora Phillips's home in Gascony; 16 cl & ccr
Josephine Ryan antiques, www.josephineryanantiques.co.uk; 16 ccl
www.les-sardines.com; 16 cr & bl The home of Fiona and Woody Woodhouse in
Herefordshire; 16 bcl Hans Blomquist and Frédérick Allouard-Rubins' home in
France; 16 bcr The home of Fiona and Woody Woodhouse in Herefordshire; 16
br Les Trois Salons, Uzès – Creators and owners Charmaine & Paul Jack; 18–19
The home of Fiona and Woody Woodhouse in Herefordshire; 20 Le Clos du
Léthé; 21 al & ar The Home of Charmaine & Paul Jack – Belvezet, France; 21 bl
The home of Fiona and Woody Woodhouse in Herefordshire; 21 br Malcolm
Gliksten's home in France; 22–23 Tania Bennett and Adrian Townsend's home in
London; 24 The Home of Charmaine & Paul Jack – Belvezet, France; 26–27 a
Les Trois Salons, Uzès – Creators and owners Charmaine & Paul Jack; 27 c
Monte-Arena, Maison d'Hotes owned by Menelik Plojoux-Demierre and Patrick
Buhler; 27 bl www.les-sardines.com; 27 br www.chambres-provence.com; 28
Les Trois Salons, Uzès – Creators and owners Charmaine & Paul Jack; 29 al
Malcolm Gliksten's home in France; 29 ar Nick & Flora Phillips's home in
Gascony; 29 b www.les-sardines.com; 30 Josephine Ryan Antiques, 63 Abbeville
Road, London SW4 9JW; 32 l Tania Bennett and Adrian Townsend's home in
London; 32 r–33 www.les-sardines.com; 34 al Hans Blomquist and Frédérick
Allouard-Rubins' home in France; 34 ar Malcolm Gliksten's home in France;
34 c The home of writer Meredith Daneman in London; 34 bl www.chambres-
provence.com; 34 br–35 Les Trois Salons, Uzès – Creators and owners
Charmaine & Paul Jack; 36–37 all www.les-sardines.com; except 37 ac Le Clos
du Léthé and 37 ar Tania Bennett and Adrian Townsend's home in London; 38
Richard Goullet Décorateur; 40–43 al Hans Blomquist and Frédérick Allouard-
Rubins' home in France; 43 ar Josephine Ryan Antiques,
www.josephineryanantiques.co.uk; 43 b The Home of Charmaine & Paul Jack –
Belvezet, France; 44 www.les-sardines.com; 45 all Richard Goullet Décorateur;
except 45 al www.chambres-provence.com; 46 Harriet Anstruther's home in
Sussex; 48 a Hans Blomquist and Frédérick Allouard-Rubins' home in France;
48 bl & bcl Tania Bennett and Adrian Townsend's home in London; 48 bcr & br
www.chambres-provence.com; 49 a & 49 bcr Nick & Flora Phillips's home in
Gascony; 49 bl The Home of Charmaine & Paul Jack – Belvezet, France; 49 bcl
Malcolm Gliksten's home in France; 49 br www.chambres-provence.com; 50–51
Les Trois Salons, Uzès – Creators and owners Charmaine & Paul Jack; 52 al
The Home of Charmaine & Paul Jack – Belvezet, France; 52 ar Hans Blomquist
and Frédérick Allouard-Rubins' home in France; 52 bl Malcolm Gliksten's home
in France; 52 br Monte-Arena, Maison d'Hotes owned by Menelik Plojoux-
Demierre and Patrick Buhler; 53 Tania Bennett and Adrian Townsend's home
in London; 54 www.chambres-provence.com; 56 Malcolm Gliksten's home in
France; 57–58 al Les Trois Salons, Uzès – Creators and owners Charmaine &
Paul Jack; 58 ar The home of Fiona and Woody Woodhouse in Herefordshire;
58 bl Josephine Ryan Antiques, www.josephineryanantiques.co.uk; 58 br
www.chambres-provence.com; 59 l Hans Blomquist and Frédérick Allouard-
Rubins' home in France; 59 r The home of Fiona and Woody Woodhouse in
Herefordshire; 60 Tania Bennett and Adrian Townsend's home in London; 62 l
Les Trois Salons, Uzès – Creators and owners Charmaine & Paul Jack; 62 ar l
Hans Blomquist and Frédérick Allouard-Rubins' home in France; 62 br Swan
House Bed & Breakfast in Hastings; 63 The home of writer Meredith Daneman
in London; 64 Hans Blomquist and Frédérick Allouard-Rubins' home in France;
65 a www.les-sardines.com; 65 c & b Josephine Ryan Antiques,
www.josephineryanantiques.co.uk; 66 l www.chambres-provence.com; 66 c
Malcolm Gliksten's home in France; 66 r The Home of Charmaine & Paul Jack –
Belvezet, France; 67 Monte-Arena, Maison d'Hotes owned by Menelik Plojoux-
Demierre and Patrick Buhler; 68–70 all Josephine Ryan Antiques,
www.josephineryanantiques.co.uk; except 70 ac Swan House Bed & Breakfast in
Hastings and 70 ar Hans Blomquist and Frédérick Allouard-Rubins' home in
France; 71 www.chambres-provence.com; 72 l Harriet Anstruther's home in
Sussex; 72 r Josephine Ryan Antiques, www.josephineryanantiques.co.uk; 73 a
Malcolm Gliksten's home in France; 73 c The Home of Charmaine & Paul Jack –
Belvezet, France; 73 cr Nick & Flora Phillips' home in Gascony; 73 b Josephine
Ryan Antiques, www.josephineryanantiques.co.uk; 74 Harriet Anstruther's home
in Sussex; 75 all The home of Fiona and Woody Woodhouse in Herefordshire;
except 75 ar Josephine Ryan Antiques, www.josephineryanantiques.co.uk; 76 l & c
The home of Fiona and Woody Woodhouse in Herefordshire; 76 r Malcolm
Gliksten's home in France; 77 al The home of Fiona and Woody Woodhouse in
Herefordshire; 77 ar Monte-Arena, Maison d'Hotes owned by Menelik Plojoux-
Demierre and Patrick Buhler; 77 bl www.chambres-provence.com; 77 br Les
Trois Salons, Uzès – Creators and owners Charmaine & Paul Jack; 80 Richard
Goullet Décorateur; 82 Hans Blomquist and Frédérick Allouard-Rubins' home
in France; 83 al www.chambres-provence.com; 83 cl & cr Hans Blomquist and
Frédérick Allouard-Rubins' home in France (Fabric angels by Hans Blomquist);
83 ar Nick & Flora Phillips' home in Gascony; 83 b Hans Blomquist and
Frédérick Allouard-Rubins' home in France; 84–85 Josephine Ryan Antiques,
www.josephineryanantiques.co.uk; 86 & 87 r Tania Bennett and Adrian
Townsend's home in London; 87 l Harriet Anstruther's home in Sussex; 88 a
www.les-sardines.com; 88 b & 89 a Harriet Anstruther's home in Sussex; 89 b
Malcolm Gliksten's home in France; 90–91 www.chambres-provence.com; 92–93
Les Trois Salons, Uzès – Creators and owners Charmaine & Paul Jack; 94–95
The Home of Charmaine & Paul Jack – Belvezet, France; 96 Le Clos du Léthé;
98 a Harriet Anstruther's home in Sussex; 98 b Hans Blomquist and Frédérick
Allouard-Rubins' home in France; 99 Josephine Ryan Antiques,
www.josephineryanantiques.co.uk; 100–101 The Home of Charmaine & Paul Jack
– Belvezet, France; 102 www.chambres-provence.com; 103–104 al The home
of writer Meredith Daneman in London; 104 b & 104–105 a Nick & Flora
Phillips's home in Gascony; 105 ar The home of writer Meredith Daneman in
London; 105 br The home of Fiona and Woody Woodhouse in Herefordshire;
106–107 Le Clos du Léthé; 108–109 Swan House Bed & Breakfast in Hastings;
110 The home of writer Meredith Daneman in London; 112–113 Tania Bennett
and Adrian Townsend's home in London; 114–115 Le Clos du Léthé; 116–117 all
Josephine Ryan Antiques, www.josephineryanantiques.co.uk; except 117 r Harriet
Anstruther's home in Sussex; 118–119 Harriet Anstruther's home in Sussex;
120 Hans Blomquist and Frédérick Allouard-Rubins' home in France; 121
www.chambres-provence.com; 122 a–123 www.les-sardines.com; 122 bl Swan
House Bed & Breakfast in Hastings; 122 br The Home of Charmaine & Paul
Jack – Belvezet, France; 124–125 Swan House Bed & Breakfast in Hastings
(walls painted by Melissa White); 126 Tania Bennett and Adrian Townsend's
home in London; 128–129 Le Clos du Léthé; 130–131 The home of writer
Meredith Daneman in London; 132 al Josephine Ryan Antiques,
www.josephineryanantiques.co.uk; 132 ar & 133 l Harriet Anstruther's home
in Sussex; 132 b Nick & Flora Phillips' home in Gascony; 133 r Malcolm
Gliksten's home in France; 134 al, ar &135 al www.les-sardines.com; 134 b
Harriet Anstruther's home in Sussex; 135 r–136 Josephine Ryan Antiques,
www.josephineryanantiques.co.uk; 138 Malcolm Gliksten's home in France; 139
Josephine Ryan Antiques, www.josephineryanantiques.co.uk; 140 www.chambres-
provence.com; 141 l Josephine Ryan Antiques, www.josephineryanantiques.co.uk;
141 r The home of Fiona and Woody Woodhouse in Herefordshire; 142 l
www.chambres-provence.com; 142 c Richard Goullet Décorateur; 142 r
The home of writer Meredith Daneman in London; 143 Swan House Bed &
Breakfast in Hastings; 144 Richard Goullet Décorateur; 146–147 all Les Trois
Salons, Uzès – Creators and owners Charmaine & Paul Jack; except 146 al &
146 cr www.chambres-provence.com and 146 ac Richard Goullet Décorateur;
148 Harriet Anstruther's home in Sussex; 149 l Richard Goullet Décorateur;
149 c & r Malcolm Gliksten's home in France; 150 al & b The Home of
Charmaine & Paul Jack – Belvezet, France; 150 ar Harriet Anstruther's home
in Sussex; 151 Richard Goullet Décorateur; 152 l www.chambres-provence.com;
152 c & r www.les-sardines.com; 153 www.les-sardines.com; 154 Nick & Flora
Phillips' home in Gascony; 157 l The home of Fiona and Woody Woodhouse in
Herefordshire; 157 c Malcolm Gliksten's home in France; 157 r Swan House
Bed & Breakfast in Hastings; 160 Harriet Anstruther's home in Sussex.

BUSINESS CREDITS

Swan House
Hill Street
Hastings TN34 3HU
+44 (0)1424 430014
res@swanhousehastings.co.uk
www.swanhousehastings.co.uk
Pages 62 br; 70 ac; 108–9; 122
bl; 124–5; 143; 157 r.

No.Eight
www.noeight.co.uk
Pages 62 br; 70 ac; 108–9; 122
bl; 124–5; 143; 157 r.

Melissa White
www.fairlyte.co.uk
Pages 124–5.

Interior Architecture &
Design – Charmaine &
Paul Jack
LESUD Design
lesudchar@wanadoo.fr
Pages 4 l, 16 acl, 16 br, 21 al &
ar, 24, 26–27 a, 28, 34 br –35,
43 b, 49 bl, 50–51, 52 al, 57–58
al, 62 l, 66 r, 73 c, 77 br, 92–93,
94–95, 100–101, 122 br,
146–147, 150 al & b.

Les Trois Salons
18 rue du Docteur-Blanchard
30700 Uzès
+33 (0)4 66 22 57 34
Pages 16 acl, 16 br, 26–27a, 28,
34 br–35, 50–51, 57–58 al, 62 l,
77 br, 92–93, 146–147.

Bexon Woodhouse Creative
+44 (0)1531 630176
+44 (0) 1531 632162
www.bexonwoodhouse.com
Pages 4 r, 14, 16 al, ar, cr, bcr
& bl, 18–19, 21 bl, 58 ar, 59 r,
75, 76 l & c, 77 al, 105 br, 141 r,
157 l.

Harriet Anstruther Design
Consultancy
+44 (0)20 7584 4776
info@harrietanstruther.com
Pages 5, 46, 72 l, 74, 87 l, 88 b
& 89 a, 98 a, 117 r, 118–119,
132 ar & 133 l, 134 b, 148, 150
ar, 160.

"La Maison"
Place de L'Eglise
30700 Blauzac
(near Uzès)
+33 (0)4 66 81 25 15
www.chambres-provence.com
Pages 6, 27 br, 34 bl, 45 al, 48
bcr & br, 49 br, 54, 58 br, 66 l,
71, 77 bl, 83 al, 90–91, 102, 121,
140, 142 l, 146 al & cr, 152 l.

"Les sardines aux yeux bleus"
(near Uzès)
+33 (0)4 66 03 10 04
contact@les-sardines.com
www.les-sardines.com
Pages 2–3, 16 ccl, 27 bl, 29 b,
32 r–33, 36–37, 44, 65 a, 88 a,
122, a–123, 134 al & ar, 135 al,
152 c & r, 153.

Relic Antiques
133–135 Pancras Road
London NW1 1UN
+44 (0)20 7485 7810
Pages 10 br, 21 br, 29 al, 34 ar,
49 bcl, 52 bl, 56, 66 c, 73 a, 76 r,
89 b, 133 r, 138, 149 c & r,
157 c.

Monte-Arena
6 Place de la Plaine
30700 Montaren (Uzès)
+33(0)4 66 03 25 24
info@monte-arena.com
www.monte-arena.com
Pages 27 c, 52 br, 67, 77 ar.

Josephine Ryan Antiques
17 Langton Street
London SW10 0JL
+44 (0)20 7352 5618
Pages, Endpapers, 1, 8–10, 11,
16 cl & ccr, 30, 43 ar, 58 bl, 65 c
& b, 68–70, 72 r, 73 b, 75 ar,
84–85, 99, 116–117, 132 al, 135
r–136, 139, 141 l.

Richard Goullet Décorateur
+33 6 51 62 64 04
www.richardgoullet-
   decoration.com
Pages 38, 45, 80, 142 c, 144,
146 ac, 149 l, 151.

Pierre Beghin
Le Clos du Léthé
Guest House – Cooking
Classes
Hameau de St Médiers
30700 Montaren et
St Médiers
France
+33 (0)4 66 74 58 37
info@closdulethe.com
www.closdulethe.com
Pages 20, 37 ac, 96, 106–107,
114–115, 128–129

INDEX

Figures in *italics* indicate photographs.

A

accessories 25, 69–77
Aga 83, *89*
Aladdin periodical 11
Alderson, Maggie 32
antiques, buying 9, 11
Antiques Trade Gazette 11
apothecary bottles *46, 65, 66*
architectural details 25–9
architectural salvage 11, 29, 132, *141*
armoires 20, 84, *84*, 87, 139
Ashwell, Rachel 22
Astier de Villatte 62, 65
Aubusson rugs 104
auctions 11

B

Baldwin, Billy 69
balustrades 25, *28–9, 107*
baskets 87, *103, 146*
bathrooms 20, *32, 34*, 127–35
    baths 128, *129, 131*, 132–3, *132–4*
    bidets 131
    underfloor heating 131
    wash-basins *46, 126, 128, 130*, 132, *133, 134*
batterie de cuisine 87
bedrooms *18–19*, 20, *110*, 111–25, *112–25*
    lighting 58, *115*
    textiles 40, *110, 112*, 116, 118, *119–23*
beds *18–19*, 115
    à la Polonaise 118
    bed hangings 116, *117*, 118
    campaign 40
    coronas 116, *117*
    headboards 118, 121
    lit bateau 118, 121, *121*
    outdoor spaces 152
    textiles *40–1*
bergère chairs 17, 101
blackboards 142
boiseries 17, *26*, 29
Boontje, Tord *115*

bottle driers *67*
boudoirs 115–16, 122
Boulesteix, Madeleine 59
boutis 40, *40*, 118, *120*
brocante 11, 17
buffets 20, *21, 75*, 84, *84*
butcher's blocks *10, 88*

C

cake stands *32*
Campbell, Nina 50
canapé 17
candlelight 55, *56–7*, 58–9, 84
carpets 104
ceramics 61–7
    colour 62–3, 65
    storage and display *21*, 62–5, *75*, 84, *84–5*, 87
    transferware 63, 65
Cézanne, Paul 71
chairs *14, 16, 17*, 20
    bergère 17, 101
    dining *82, 83, 83*, 84
    fauteuil 17, *18–19, 23*, 84, *106*
    living rooms 101, 104
    sièges courants 101, 104
    sièges meublants 27, 101
    sièges voyants 27, 101
chaise longues 20
chambre à coucher 116, 122
chandeliers 55, *58–9, 74*, 84, *91, 102*
chicken-wire cupboard doors 20, *21*, 87
Chinoiserie *77*, 116
chocolatier's tables *82*
clocks 77
collections, making and displaying 69–77
colour 25, 31–7
    bedrooms 116
    dados *32–3, 36–7, 88, 123*
    distressed 31
    garden furniture 149
    Gustavian style *32–3*, 36

paintwork 29, *29*, 31–6
    tableware 62, 65
    textiles 40, 44
    two-tone schemes *33*
commodes *20*
computers 139
concrete 87, 90, *95*, 135
Conor, Lin 59
Cornell, Joseph 71
coronas 116, *117*
curtains 40, *44–5*, 83, 131
    doors *44, 45, 147*
    windows 106, 122

D

dados *32–3, 36–7, 88*, 123
demi-lune tables *141*
dépot-ventes 11
desks *138*
dining outdoors 149
dining rooms 20, *23*, 80, *82–3*, 83–4, 90, *90–3*
    tableware 61–7
    displaying collections 68–77, *69–77, 85*
    ceramics *21*, 62–5, *75*
    glass *21*, 65, *66–7*
    pictures 46–53, *48–9, 73, 74, 76*
    textiles *42–3, 75*
distressing 31
door furniture 25, *27*
doors 29, 31, *57*, 146–7
    curtains *44, 45, 147*
draper's cabinet *141*

E

EBay, purchasing on 11

F

faience 62, 65
fairground art *66*
Faisaille pots *64*
fauteuil chair 17, *18–19, 23*, 84, *106*
Feng Shui 72

Fierard, Clementine 10
fireplaces 27, 29, *37*, 142
    kitchens and dining rooms 87, *87, 88*, 91
    living rooms 101, *101, 105, 109*
    Louis XV *26*
    woodburning stoves 101, *101*
flea markets 11, 17
floors 29, *37, 45*, 102
fonts *147*
Fontainebleau 115
foxing 50, *116*
frames *73, 76*
fresco secco *124–5*
friperie 11
furniture 15–23
    distressing 31
    outdoor spaces 56, *144, 145, 148*, 149, *150–3*, 152
    paintwork *16, 17*, 20, 22
    reproduction 22, *106*
    upholstery *16, 18–19*, 20

G

garde manger 20
gardens *see* outdoor spaces
glass 61–7
    chandeliers 55, *58–9*
    colour 62–3
    storage and display *21*, 65, *66–7*, 84, *84–5, 86*, 87
Gustavian style *32–3*, 36

H

halls *47, 57*
headboards 118, 121
Hicks, David, tablescapes 72, 76
Huet, Christophe 39
humour, use of 72

I

'Indiennes' 39, 40
internet, purchasing on 11
ironwork 29

J

Journal of Antiques 11

K

kilims 45, 194
Kira, Alexander 128
kitchens 20, 32, 80–95, 81, 83–4, 94–5
storage and display 20, 21, 62–3

L

lead crystal 55
Levée 115
lighting 55–9
bedrooms 58, 115
candles 55, 56–7, 58–9, 84
chandeliers 55, 58–9, 84, 91, 102
kitchens and dining rooms 84
lamps 45, 58
Lille 11
lit bateau 118, 121, 121
living rooms 96, 97–109, 98–109
Louis Quinze 17, 23, 26

M

marble 20, 82, 103, 133
floors 104
Marie Antoinette 39, 152
marquise 20
Maugham, Syrie 22
mezzanines 107
mirrors 27, 46–53, 46, 50–1, 52, 53, 82, 152
foxed 50, 116
marble frames 103
trumeau 10, 27

verre églomisé 50
monograms 40, 122
Morandi, Giorgio 36, 53, 71
muslin 117, 119

O

Oberkampf, Christophe-Philippe 39
outdoor spaces 73, 145–52, 146–53
furniture 144, 145, 148, 149, 150–3, 152
mirrors, use of 50, 152, 153
paintwork 31, 34, 146–7

P

paintwork
colour 29, 29, 31–6
dados 32–3, 36–7, 88, 123
distressed 31
fresco secco 124–5
furniture 16, 17, 20, 22
garden furniture 149
mirror and picture frames 47, 73
outside walls 31, 34, 146–7
panelling 17, 26, 26–7, 29, 108–9, 141
painted 34
tongue-and-groove 134
see also boiseries
Paris 11
Paris dust 149
parquet floors 29
passementerie 45
paths 149, 152
patisserie 87
paving 29
Petit Trianon 152
pewter 10
pictures 46–53, 48–9, 73, 74, 76, 84
pin boards 141, 142
Les Puces 11

Q

quilts 40, 40, 41, 116, 118

R

Rambouillet, Marquise de 115
Rococo style 115
room layout 25–7
Rozot, Isabelle 20
rugs 45, 104, 109
Ryan, Josephine 8–9, 10, 11, 53

S

Sacchi, Jane 40
secretaires 138
sheds as workspaces 142
sheets 40, 42, 131, 147
monogrammed 40, 122
shelves 62–3, 65, 85, 86, 87
shelf frills 43
shutters 25, 34, 56, 106, 122
sièges courants 101, 104
sièges meublants 27, 101
sièges voyants 27, 101
silver 10, 71, 91
Silvestrin, Claudio 132
sinks 83, 85, 88
Smith, Paul 17
sofas 17, 20, 23, 84, 98, 101, 104, 105, 108–9
stairways 24, 28–9, 29, 107
Starck, Philippe, 'Ghost' chair 17
statues 10, 70, 75, 135
symmetry 72, 104

T

tableware 61–7, 84, 93
see also ceramics; glass
terracotta 29, 37, 87, 104, 131, 152
textiles 25, 39–45
bedrooms 40, 110, 112, 116, 118, 119–23
colour 40, 44

display 42–3, 75
'Indiennes' 39, 40
muslin 117, 119
texture 116
ticking 40, 44, 83
toiles de jouy 39–40, 121–2
as wall treatment 40, 121–2
texture 95, 108–9
tiles 29, 37, 45, 102, 104, 133, 135, 152
Timorous Beasties 40
toiles de jouy 39–40, 121–2
trumeau mirrors 10, 27

U

underfloor heating 131
upholstery 16, 18–19
furniture 20

V

Van Severen, Maarten 17
verre églomisé 50
Versailles 39, 115
vide-grenier 11

W

walls
dados 32–3, 36–7, 88, 123
fresco secco 124–5
outside walls 31, 34
textile-covered 40, 121–2
wallpaper 112–13, 115, 116
Windham, Donald 71
windows 25, 31, 34, 65, 66
curtains 40, 106, 122
shutters 25, 34, 56, 106, 122
wine tasting tables 73
wirework 91
Wolfe, Elsie de 22
woodburning stoves 101, 101
workrooms 136, 137–43, 138–43

ACKNOWLEDGMENTS

Thank you to everyone who made this book possible, particularly to Jess Walton for suggesting it, Claire Richardson for shooting it and especially to Hilary Robertson for writing it. Thanks also to all of those at Ryland Peters & Small who helped bring it all together into its finished form. To those of you who opened up your homes and allowed me to come in and rearrange your furniture, thank you for your patience and hospitality. Thank you to Gosia and Colette, my right-hand women.

A special thank you to my family — Mohit, Cahal and Uma Rose — who allow me to hop across the Channel to France for my endless shopping jaunts.

Josephine Ryan

Josephine Ryan has developed a signature style that is always fresh, innovative and inspiring; at last you can see how she puts it all together in a book! Claire Richardson's pictures perfectly capture the subtlety and complexity of Jo's vision of the world.

I'd like to thank the Ryland Peters & Small team for their help and support, the internet cafes of New York, particularly Smooch, for providing desk space, occasional distraction and delicious coffee, and the beautiful library at the Pratt Institute for allowing me to use their resources.

And, of course, thanks to my family — Al and Gus and the indispensible Christie — for their patience while I dreamed of France.

Hilary Robertson